MznLnx

Missing Links Exam Preps

Exam Prep for

Partial Differential Equations: Analytical and Numerical Methods

Gockenbach, 1st Edition

The MznLnx Exam Prep is your link from the texbook and lecture to your exams.

The MznLnx Exam Preps are unauthorized and comprehensive reviews of your textbooks.

MznLnx

Rico
Publications

Exam Prep for Partial Differential Equations: Analytical and Numerical Methods
1st Edition
Gockenbach

Publisher: Raymond Houge

Assistant Editor: Michael Rouger

Text and Cover Designer: Lisa Buckner

Marketing Manager: Sara Swagger

Project Manager, Editorial Production: Jerry Emerson

Art Director: Vernon Lowerui

Product Manager: Dave Mason

Editorial Assitant: Rachel Guzmanji

Pedagogy: Debra Long

Cover Image: Jim Reed/Getty Images

Text and Cover Printer: City Printing, Inc.

Compositor: Media Mix, Inc.

Printed in the United States
ISBN:

For more information about our products, contact us at:

Dave.Mason@RicoPublications.com

For permission to use material from this text or

product, submit a request online to:

Dave.Mason@RicoPublications.com

Contents

TO THE STUDENT

COMPREHENSIVE

The *MznLnx* Exam Prep series is designed to help you pass your exams. Editors at MznLnx review your textbooks and then prepare these practice exams to help you master the textbook material. Unlike study guides, workbooks, and practice tests provided by the texbook publisher and textbook authors, *MznLnx* gives you **all** of the material in each chapter in exam form, not just samples, so you can be sure to nail your exam.

MECHANICAL

The MznLnx Exam Prep series creates exams that will help you learn the subject matter as well as test you on your understanding. Each question is designed to help you master the concept. Just working through the exams, you gain an understanding of the subject--its a simple mechanical process that produces success.

INTEGRATED STUDY GUIDE AND REVIEW

MznLnx is not just a set of exams designed to test you, its also a comprehensive review of the subject content. Each exam question is also a review of the concept, making sure that you will get the answer correct without having to go to other sources of material. You learn as you go! Its the easiest way to pass an exam.

HUMOR

Studying can be tedious and dry. MznLnx's instructional design includes moderate humor within the exam questions on occassion, to break the tedium and revitalize the brain

1. Suppose that φ : M → N is a smooth map between smooth manifolds; then the _____ of φ at a point x is, in some sense, the best linear approximation of φ near x. It can be viewed as generalization of the total derivative of ordinary calculus. Explicitly, it is a linear map from the tangent space of M at x to the tangent space of N at φ

    a. Concurrent
    b. Grill
    c. Differential
    d. Boundary

2. _____s arise in many problems in physics, engineering, etc. The following examples show how to solve _____s in a few simple cases when an exact solution exists.

    A separable linear ordinary _____ of the first order has the general form:

    $$\frac{dy}{dt} + f(t)y = 0$$

    where f is some known function.

    a. Nahm equations
    b. Homogeneous differential equation
    c. Nullcline
    d. Differential equation

3. In mathematics, an _____ in the sense of ring theory is a subring $\mathcal{O}$ of a ring R that satisfies the conditions

    1. R is a ring which is a finite-dimensional algebra over the rational number field $\mathbb{Q}$
    2. $\mathcal{O}$ spans R over $\mathbb{Q}$, so that $\mathbb{Q}\mathcal{O} = R$, and
    3. $\mathcal{O}$ is a lattice in R.

    The third condition can be stated more accurately, in terms of the extension of scalars of R to the real numbers, embedding R in a real vector space. In less formal terms, additively $\mathcal{O}$ should be a free abelian group generated by a basis for R over $\mathbb{Q}$.

    The leading example is the case where R is a number field K and $\mathcal{O}$ is its ring of integers. In algebraic number theory there are examples for any K other than the rational field of proper subrings of the ring of integers that are also _____s.

    a. Algebraic
    b. Order
    c. Annihilator
    d. Efficiency

4. In mathematics, a _____ is a system which is not linear. Less technically, a _____ is any problem where the variabl to be solved for cannot be written as a linear sum of independent components. A nonhomogenous system, which is linear apart from the presence of a function of the independent variables, is nonlinear according to a strict definition, but such systems are usually studied alongside linear systems, because they can be transformed to a linear system as long as a particular solution is known.

a. Nonlinear system
c. 1-center problem

b. George Dantzig
d. Metric system

5.   In mathematics, a _____ is a constant multiplicative factor of a certain object. For example, in the expression $9x^2$, the _____ of x^2 is 9.

The object can be such things as a variable, a vector, a function, etc.

a. Multivariate division algorithm
c. Stability radius

b. Fibonacci polynomials
d. Coefficient

6.   In mathematics, _____s is a term applied to differential operators, and also some difference operators, to signify that they contain no functions of the independent variables, other than constant functions. In other words, it singles out special operators, within the larger class of operators having variable coefficients. Such _____ operators have been found to be the easiest to handle, in several respects.

a. Semi-elliptic operator
c. Constant coefficient

b. Peetre theorem
d. Laplace-Beltrami operator

1. The _____ is an important partial differential equation which describes the distribution of heat in a given region over time. For a function u

$$\frac{\partial u}{\partial t} - k \left(\frac{\partial^2 u}{\partial x^2} + \frac{\partial^2 u}{\partial y^2} + \frac{\partial^2 u}{\partial z^2} \right) = 0$$

where k is a constant.

The _____ is of fundamental importance in diverse scientific fields.

a. 120-cell

b. 1-center problem

c. Heat equation

d. 2-3 heap

2. In mathematics, a _____ is a vector space of functions equipped with a norm that is a combination of L^p norms of the function itself as well as its derivatives up to a given order. The derivatives are understood in a suitable weak sense to make the space complete, thus a Banach space. Intuitively, a _____ is a Banach space or Hilbert space of functions with sufficiently many derivatives for some application domain, such as partial differential equations, and equipped with a norm that measures both the size and smoothness of a function.

a. 1-center problem

b. 2-3 heap

c. 120-cell

d. Sobolev space

3. The _____ of a material is defined as its mass per unit volume:

$$\rho = \frac{m}{V}$$

Different materials usually have different densities, so _____ is an important concept regarding buoyancy, metal purity and packaging.

In some cases _____ is expressed as the dimensionless quantities specific gravity or relative _____, in which case it is expressed in multiples of the _____ of some other standard material, usually water or air.

In a well-known story, Archimedes was given the task of determining whether King Hiero's goldsmith was embezzling gold during the manufacture of a wreath dedicated to the gods and replacing it with another, cheaper alloy.

a. 2-3 heap

b. 120-cell

c. 1-center problem

d. Density

4. In mathematics, the _____, name after Ivar Fredholm, is one of Fredholm's theorems and is a result in Fredholm theory. It may be expressed in several ways, as a theorem of linear algebra, a theorem of integral equations, or as a theorem on Fredholm operators. Part of the result states that, a non-zero complex number in the spectrum of a compact operator is an eigenvalue.

a. Fredholm integral equation
c. Liouville-Neumann series

b. Fredholm operator
d. Fredholm alternative

5. _____ is a branch of mathematics that includes the study of limits, derivatives, integrals, and infinite series, and constitutes a major part of modern university education. Historically, it has been referred to as 'the _____ of infinitesimals', or 'infinitesimal _____'. Most basically, _____ is the study of change, in the same way that geometry is the study of space.

a. Calculus
c. Test for Divergence

b. Hyperbolic angle
d. Partial sum

6. In the various subfields of physics, there exist two common usages of the term _____, both with rigorous mathematical frameworks.

- In the study of transport phenomena, _____ is defined as the amount that flows through a unit area per unit time. _____ in this definition is a vector.
- In the field of electromagnetism, _____ is usually the integral of a vector quantity over a finite surface. The result of this integration is a scalar quantity. The magnetic _____ is thus the integral of the magnetic vector field B over a surface, and the electric _____ is defined similarly. Using this definition, the _____ of the Poynting vector over a specified surface is the rate at which electromagnetic energy flows through that surface. Confusingly, the Poynting vector is sometimes called the power _____, which is an example of the first usage of _____, above. It has units of watts per square metre

One could argue, based on the work of James Clerk Maxwell, that the transport definition precedes the more recent way the term is used in electromagnetism. The specific quote from Maxwell is 'In the case of _____es, we have to take the integral, over a surface, of the _____ through every element of the surface. The result of this operation is called the surface integral of the _____.

a. Flux
c. 120-cell

b. Rotational speed
d. 1-center problem

7. The _____ specifies the relationship between the two central operations of calculus, differentiation and integration.

The first part of the theorem, sometimes called the first _____, shows that an indefinite integration can be reversed by a differentiation.

The second part, sometimes called the second _____, allows one to compute the definite integral of a function by using any one of its infinitely many antiderivatives.

a. Maxima and minima
c. Hyperbolic angle

b. Standard part function
d. Fundamental theorem of calculus

8. In commutative algebra, the notions of an element _____ over a ring, and of an _____ extension of rings, are a generalization of the notions in field theory of an element being algebraic over a field, and of an algebraic extension of fields.

The special case of greatest interest in number theory is that of complex numbers _____ over the ring of integers Z.

The term ring will be understood to mean commutative ring with a unit.

a. Arc length
b. Integral test for convergence
c. Antidifferentiation
d. Integral

9. In mathematics, a _____ is a statement that can be proved on the basis of explicitly stated or previously agreed assumptions.
a. Disjunction introduction
b. Logical value
c. Theorem
d. Boolean function

10. In vector calculus, the _____ of a scalar field is a vector field which points in the direction of the greatest rate of increase of the scalar field, and whose magnitude is the greatest rate of change.

A generalization of the _____ for functions on a Euclidean space which have values in another Euclidean space is the Jacobian. A further generalization for a function from one Banach space to another is the Fréchet derivative.

a. Directional derivative
b. Stationary point
c. Metric derivative
d. Gradient

11. In plumbing, a _____ or basin is a bowl-shaped fixture that is used for washing hands or small objects such as food, dishes, nylons, socks or underwear. In American plumbing parlance, a bathroom _____ is known as a lavatory.

_____s generally have taps that supply hot and cold water and may include a spray feature to be used for faster rinsing.

a. 2-3 heap
b. 120-cell
c. 1-center problem
d. Sink

12. In physics, _____, k, is the property of a material that indicates its ability to conduct heat. It appears primarily in Fourier's Law for heat conduction.

First, we define heat conduction by the formula:

$$H = \frac{\Delta Q}{\Delta t} = k \times A \times \frac{\Delta T}{x}$$

where $\frac{\Delta Q}{\Delta t}$ is the rate of heat flow, k is the _____, A is the total cross sectional area of conducting surface, ΔT is temperature difference and x is the thickness of conducting surface separating the 2 temperatures.

a. 1-center problem

b. 2-3 heap

c. Thermal conductivity

d. 120-cell

13.   In topology, the _____ of a subset S of a topological space X is the set of points which can be approached both from S and from the outside of S. More formally, it is the set of points in the closure of S, not belonging to the interior of S. An element of the _____ of S is called a _____ point of S.

a. Heap

b. Boundary

c. Character

d. Bertrand paradox

14.   In mathematics, in the field of differential equations, a _____ is a differential equation together with a set of additional restraints, called the boundary conditions. A solution to a _____ is a solution to the differential equation which also satisfies the boundary conditions.

_____s arise in several branches of physics as any physical differential equation will have them.

a. Normal mode

b. Separation of variables

c. Riccati equation

d. Boundary value problem

15.   Initial objects are also called _____, and terminal objects are also called final.

a. Direct limit

b. Terminal object

c. Colimit

d. Coterminal

16.   The requirement that L have strictly positive diagonal entries can be dropped to extend the factorization to the positive semidefinite case. The statement then reads: a square matrix A has a Cholesky decomposition if and only if A is Hermitian and positive semi-definite. _____ for positive semidefinite matrices are not unique in general.

a. Cholesky factorizations

b. Wold decomposition

c. Singular values

d. Positive definite kernel

17.   In chemistry, _____ is the measure of how much of a given substance there is mixed with another substance. This can apply to any sort of chemical mixture, but most frequently the concept is limited to homogeneous solutions, where it refers to the amount of solute in the solvent.

To concentrate a solution, one must add more solute, or reduce the amount of solvent (for instance, by selective evaporation.)

a. 1-center problem

b. Concentration

c. 2-3 heap

d. 120-cell

18.   In mathematics, a _____ is a constant multiplicative factor of a certain object. For example, in the expression $9x^2$, the _____ of x^2 is 9.

The object can be such things as a variable, a vector, a function, etc.

a. Fibonacci polynomials

b. Multivariate division algorithm

c. Stability radius

d. Coefficient

19. The _____ is a partial differential equation which describes density fluctuations in a material undergoing diffusion. It is also used to describe processes exhibiting diffusive-like behaviour, for instance the 'diffusion' of alleles in a population in population genetics.

The equation is usually written as:

$$\frac{\partial \phi(\vec{r}, t)}{\partial t} = \nabla \cdot \left(D(\phi, \vec{r}) \, \nabla \phi(\vec{r}, t) \right),$$

where $\phi(\vec{r}, t)$ is the density of the diffusing material at location $\vec{r}$ and time t and $D(\phi, \vec{r})$ is the collective diffusion coefficient for density φ at location $\vec{r}$; the nabla symbol ∇ represents the vector differential operator del acting on the space coordinates.

a. 2-3 heap

b. Diffusion equation

c. 1-center problem

d. 120-cell

20. In mathematics, in the field of differential equations, a boundary value problem is a differential equation together with a set of additional restraints, called the _____. A solution to a boundary value problem is a solution to the differential equation which also satisfies the _____.

Boundary value problems arise in several branches of physics as any physical differential equation will have them.

a. Total differential equation

b. Boundary value problem

c. Separation of variables

d. Boundary conditions

21. In mathematical analysis, the _____ is the collection of functions

$$D_n(x) = \sum_{k=-n}^{n} e^{ikx} = 1 + 2 \sum_{k=1}^{n} \cos(kx) = \frac{\sin\left(\left(n + \frac{1}{2}\right) x\right)}{\sin(x/2)}.$$

It is named after Johann Peter Gustav Lejeune Dirichlet.

The importance of the _____ comes from its relation to Fourier series. The convolution of D_nπ is the nth-degree Fourier series approximation to f.

a. Total variation

b. Constructive analysis

c. Mountain pass theorem

d. Dirichlet kernel

22. The mathematical concept of a _____ expresses the intuitive idea of deterministic dependence between two quantities, one of which is viewed as primary and the other as secondary. A _____ then is a way to associate a unique output for each input of a specified type, for example, a real number or an element of a given set.

a. Grill   b. Going up
c. Coherent   d. Function

23.   In the various branches of mathematics that fall under the heading of abstract algebra, the _____ of a homomorphism measures the degree to which the homomorphism fails to be injective. An important special case is the _____ of a matrix, also called the null space.

The definition of _____ takes various forms in various contexts.

a. Leibniz formula   b. Kernel
c. Constructivism   d. Bertrand paradox

24.   In mathematics, an _____ is a statement about the relative size or order of two objects, or about whether they are the same or not

- The notation a < b means that a is less than b.
- The notation a > b means that a is greater than b.
- The notation a ≠ b means that a is not equal to b, but does not say that one is bigger than the other or even that they can be compared in size.

In all these cases, a is not equal to b, hence, '_____'.

These relations are known as strict _____

- The notation a ≤ b means that a is less than or equal to b;
- The notation a ≥ b means that a is greater than or equal to b;

An additional use of the notation is to show that one quantity is much greater than another, normally by several orders of magnitude.

- The notation a << b means that a is much less than b.
- The notation a >> b means that a is much greater than b.

If the sense of the _____ is the same for all values of the variables for which its members are defined, then the _____ is called an 'absolute' or 'unconditional' _____. If the sense of an _____ holds only for certain values of the variables involved, but is reversed or destroyed for other values of the variables, it is called a conditional _____.

An _____ may appear unsolvable because it only states whether a number is larger or smaller than another number; but it is possible to apply the same operations for equalities to inequalities. For example, to find x for the _____ 10x > 23 one would divide 23 by 10.

a. Inequality   b. A chemical equation
c. A posteriori   d. A Mathematical Theory of Communication

25. The _____ , is achieved in a packed stadium when successive groups of spectators briefly stand and raise their arms. Each spectator is required to rise at the same time as those straight in front and behind, and slightly after the person immediately to either the right or the left. Immediately upon stretching to full height, the spectator returns to the usual seated position.
    a. Wave
    c. Pauli exclusion principle
    b. Thermodynamic limit
    d. Lagrangian

26. The _____ is an important second-order linear partial differential equation that describes the propagation of a variety of waves, such as sound waves, light waves and water waves. It arises in fields such as acoustics, electromagnetics, and fluid dynamics. Historically, the problem of a vibrating string such as that of a musical instrument was studied by Jean le Rond d'Alembert, Leonhard Euler, Daniel Bernoulli, and Joseph-Louis Lagrange.
    a. Random walk
    c. Wave equation
    b. Lagrangian
    d. Cauchy momentum equation

27. _____ is the lethal suspension of a person by a ligature. The Oxford English Dictionary states that _____ in this sense is 'specifically to put to death by suspension by the neck', although it formerly also referred to crucifixion.

The preferred past tense and past participle in English is hanged, not 'hung'.

    a. 120-cell
    c. 2-3 heap
    b. Hanging
    d. 1-center problem

28. _____ is an important second-order linear partial differential equation that describes the propagation of a variety of waves, such as sound waves, light waves and water waves. It arises in fields such as acoustics, electromagnetics, and fluid dynamics. Historically, the problem of a vibrating string such as that of a musical instrument was studied by Jean le Rond d'Alembert, Leonhard Euler, Daniel Bernoulli, and Joseph-Louis Lagrange.
    a. Cauchy momentum equation
    c. Geodesic
    b. Dispersion relations
    d. The wave equation

29. The _____ (symbol: N) is the SI derived unit of force, named after Isaac _____ in recognition of his work on classical mechanics.

The _____ is the unit of force derived in the SI system; it is equal to the amount of force required to accelerate a mass of one kilogram at a rate of one meter per second per second. Algebraically:

$$1 \text{ N} = 1 \ \frac{\text{kg} \cdot \text{m}}{\text{s}^2}.$$

- 1 N is the force of Earth's gravity on an object with a mass of about 102 g ($\frac{1}{9.8}$ kg) (such as a small apple.)
- On Earth's surface, a mass of 1 kg exerts a force of approximately 9.80665 N [down] (or 1 kgf.) The approximation of 1 kg corresponding to 10 N is sometimes used as a rule of thumb in everyday life and in engineering.
- The force of Earth's gravity on a human being with a mass of 70 kg is approximately 687 N.
- The dot product of force and distance is mechanical work. Thus, in SI units, a force of 1 N exerted over a distance of 1 m is 1 NÂ·m of work. The Work-Energy Theorem states that the work done on a body is equal to the change in energy of the body. 1 NÂ·m = 1 J (joule), the SI unit of energy.
- It is common to see forces expressed in kilonewtons or kN, where 1 kN = 1 000 N.

a. 2-3 heap   b. Newton
c. 1-center problem   d. 120-cell

30.   The _____, denoted G, is an empirical physical constant involved in the calculation of the gravitational attraction between objects with mass. It appears in Newton's law of universal gravitation and in Einstein's theory of general relativity. It is also known as the universal _____, Newton's constant, and colloquially Big G.
a. Circular orbit   b. Major axis
c. Semi-major axis   d. Gravitational constant

31.   A vibration in a string is a wave. Usually a _____ produces a sound whose frequency in most cases is constant. Therefore, since frequency characterizes the pitch, the sound produced is a constant note.
a. 120-cell   b. Harmonic oscillator
c. 1-center problem   d. Vibrating string

1. In mathematical analysis, the _____ is the collection of functions

$$D_n(x) = \sum_{k=-n}^{n} e^{ikx} = 1 + 2\sum_{k=1}^{n} \cos(kx) = \frac{\sin\left(\left(n+\frac{1}{2}\right)x\right)}{\sin(x/2)}.$$

It is named after Johann Peter Gustav Lejeune Dirichlet.

The importance of the _____ comes from its relation to Fourier series. The convolution of $D_n\pi$ is the nth-degree Fourier series approximation to f.

    a. Constructive analysis   b. Total variation
    c. Dirichlet kernel   d. Mountain pass theorem

2. In mathematics, the _____, name after Ivar Fredholm, is one of Fredholm's theorems and is a result in Fredholm theory. It may be expressed in several ways, as a theorem of linear algebra, a theorem of integral equations, or as a theorem on Fredholm operators. Part of the result states that, a non-zero complex number in the spectrum of a compact operator is an eigenvalue.

    a. Fredholm integral equation   b. Liouville-Neumann series
    c. Fredholm operator   d. Fredholm alternative

3. In mathematics, the _____ or Pythagoras' theorem is a relation in Euclidean geometry among the three sides of a right triangle. The theorem is named after the Greek mathematician Pythagoras, who by tradition is credited with its discovery and proof, although it is often argued that knowledge of the theory predates him.. The theorem is as follows:

In any right triangle, the area of the square whose side is the hypotenuse is equal to the sum of the areas of the squares whose sides are the two legs.

    a. 120-cell   b. Pythagorean theorem
    c. 1-center problem   d. 2-3 heap

4. In mathematics, a _____ is a vector space of functions equipped with a norm that is a combination of L^p norms of the function itself as well as its derivatives up to a given order. The derivatives are understood in a suitable weak sense to make the space complete, thus a Banach space. Intuitively, a _____ is a Banach space or Hilbert space of functions with sufficiently many derivatives for some application domain, such as partial differential equations, and equipped with a norm that measures both the size and smoothness of a function.

    a. 2-3 heap   b. 120-cell
    c. 1-center problem   d. Sobolev space

5. In abstract algebra, a field extension L /K is called _____ if every element of L is _____ over K. Field extensions which are not _____.

For example, the field extension R/Q, that is the field of real numbers as an extension of the field of rational numbers, is transcendental, while the field extensions C/R and Q

a. Ideal
c. Identity

b. Echo
d. Algebraic

6.   In mathematics, especially in the area of abstract algebra known as ring theory, a _____ is a ring with 0 ≠ 1 such that ab = 0 implies that either a = 0 or b = 0. That is, it is a nontrivial ring without left or right zero divisors. A commutative _____ is called an integral _____.

a. Simple ring
c. Left primitive ring

b. Modular representation theory
d. Domain

7.   The mathematical concept of a _____ expresses the intuitive idea of deterministic dependence between two quantities, one of which is viewed as primary and the other as secondary. A _____ then is a way to associate a unique output for each input of a specified type, for example, a real number or an element of a given set.

a. Going up
c. Coherent

b. Grill
d. Function

8.   In commutative algebra, the notions of an element _____ over a ring, and of an _____ extension of rings, are a generalization of the notions in field theory of an element being algebraic over a field, and of an algebraic extension of fields.

The special case of greatest interest in number theory is that of complex numbers _____ over the ring of integers Z.

The term ring will be understood to mean commutative ring with a unit.

a. Integral test for convergence
c. Antidifferentiation

b. Arc length
d. Integral

9.   In the various branches of mathematics that fall under the heading of abstract algebra, the _____ of a homomorphism measures the degree to which the homomorphism fails to be injective. An important special case is the _____ of a matrix, also called the null space.

The definition of _____ takes various forms in various contexts.

a. Bertrand paradox
c. Constructivism

b. Kernel
d. Leibniz formula

10.   In mathematics, a linear map is a function between two vector spaces that preserves the operations of vector addition and scalar multiplication. The expression '_____' is in especially common use, for linear maps from a vector space to itself In advanced mathematics, the definition of linear function coincides with the definition of linear map.

a. Morphism
c. Morphisms

b. Hubbard-Stratonovich transformation
d. Linear operator

11.   A _____ is a mathematical model of a system based on the use of a linear operator. _____s typically exhibit features and properties that are much simpler than the general, nonlinear case. As a mathematical abstraction or idealization, _____s find important applications in automatic control theory, signal processing, and telecommunications.

a. Hybrid system

b. Percolation

c. Predispositioning Theory

d. Linear system

12. In mathematics, a _____ is a rectangular table of elements, which may be numbers or, more generally, any abstract quantities that can be added and multiplied. Matrices are used to describe linear equations, keep track of the coefficients of linear transformations and to record data that depend on multiple parameters. Matrices are described by the field of _____ theory.

a. Double counting

b. Coherent

c. Compression

d. Matrix

13. In physics, an _____ is a function acting on the space of physical states. As a result of its application on a physical state, another physical state is obtained, very often along with some extra relevant information.

The simplest example of the utility of _____s is the study of symmetry.

a. Affine Hecke algebra

b. Algebraic signal processing

c. Operand

d. Operator

14. In descriptive statistics, the _____ is the length of the smallest interval which contains all the data. It is calculated by subtracting the smallest observations from the greatest and provides an indication of statistical dispersion.

It is measured in the same units as the data.

a. Bandwidth

b. Range

c. Kernel

d. Class

15. In mathematics, a _____ is a statement that can be proved on the basis of explicitly stated or previously agreed assumptions.

a. Logical value

b. Theorem

c. Disjunction introduction

d. Boolean function

16. In physics and in _____ calculus, a _____ is a concept characterized by a magnitude and a direction. A _____ can be thought of as an arrow in Euclidean space, drawn from an initial point A pointing to a terminal point B.

a. Dominance

b. Constraint

c. Deviation

d. Vector

17. The requirement that L have strictly positive diagonal entries can be dropped to extend the factorization to the positive semidefinite case. The statement then reads: a square matrix A has a Cholesky decomposition if and only if A is Hermitian and positive semi-definite. _____ for positive semidefinite matrices are not unique in general.

a. Singular values

b. Wold decomposition

c. Cholesky factorizations

d. Positive definite kernel

18. In mathematical analysis, a _____ is a classification of functions according to the properties of their derivatives. Higher order _____es correspond to the existence of more derivatives. Functions that have derivatives of all orders are called smooth.

a. Metric derivative

b. Directional derivative

c. Logarithmic derivative

d. Differentiability class

19.   of the difference quotient as h approaches zero, if this limit exists. If the limit exists, then f is _____ at a. Here f′ (a) is one of several common notations for the derivative

a. 2-3 heap

b. 1-center problem

c. 120-cell

d. Differentiable

20.   In mathematics, a _____ is a set of functions of a given kind from a set X to a set Y. It is called a space because in many applications, it is a topological space or a vector space or both.

_____s appear in various areas of mathematics:

- in set theory, the power set of a set X may be identified with the set of all functions from X to {0,1};, denoted 2^X. More generally, the set of functions X → Y is denoted Y^X.

- in linear algebra the set of all linear transformations from a vector space V to another one, W, over the same field, is itself a vector space;

- in functional analysis the same is seen for continuous linear transformations, including topologies on the vector spaces in the above, and many of the major examples are _____s carrying a topology; the best known examples include Hilbert spaces and Banach spaces.

- in functional analysis the set of all functions from the natural numbers to some set X is called a sequence space. It consists of the set of all possible sequences of elements of X.

a. Mackey-Arens theorem

b. Strong operator topology

c. Weak topology

d. Function space

21.   In mathematics, a _____ is a system which is not linear. Less technically, a _____ is any problem where the variabl to be solved for cannot be written as a linear sum of independent components. A nonhomogenous system, which is linear apart from the presence of a function of the independent variables, is nonlinear according to a strict definition, but such systems are usually studied alongside linear systems, because they can be transformed to a linear system as long as a particular solution is known.

a. George Dantzig

b. 1-center problem

c. Metric system

d. Nonlinear system

22.   _____ is a fundamental construction of differential calculus and admits many possible generalizations within the fields of mathematical analysis, combinatorics, algebra, and geometry.

In real, complex, and functional analysis, _____s are generalized to functions of several real or complex variables and functions between topological vector spaces. An important case is the variational _____ in the calculus of variations.

a. Derivative

b. Lin-Tsien equation

c. Functional derivative

d. Metric derivative

23.   Suppose that φ : M → N is a smooth map between smooth manifolds; then the _____ of φ at a point x is, in some sense, the best linear approximation of φ near x. It can be viewed as generalization of the total derivative of ordinary calculus. Explicitly, it is a linear map from the tangent space of M at x to the tangent space of N at φ

a. Grill

b. Concurrent

c. Boundary

d. Differential

24.   In mathematics, the term _____ is frequently used for objects (for examples, groups or topological spaces) that have a very simple structure. For non-mathematicians, they are sometimes more difficult to visualize or understand than other, more complicated objects.

Examples include:

- empty set: the set containing no members
- _____ group: the mathematical group containing only the identity element
- _____ ring: a ring defined on a singleton set.

_____ also refers to solutions to an equation that have a very simple structure, but for the sake of completeness cannot be omitted. These solutions are called the _____ solution.

a. Well-defined

b. Pure mathematics

c. Per mil

d. Trivial

25.   In linear algebra, _____ is an efficient algorithm for solving systems of linear equations, finding the rank of a matrix, and calculating the inverse of an invertible square matrix. _____ is named after German mathematician and scientist Carl Friedrich Gauss.

Elementary row operations are used to reduce a matrix to row echelon form.

a. Crout matrix decomposition

b. Cholesky decomposition

c. Gaussian elimination

d. Conjugate gradient method

26.   In mathematics, the _____ is an operation which takes two vectors over the real numbers R and returns a real-valued scalar quantity. It is the standard inner product of the orthonormal Euclidean space.

The _____ of two vectors a = [a_1, a_2, â€¦ , a_n] and b = [b_1, b_2, â€¦ , b_n] is defined as:

$$\mathbf{a} \cdot \mathbf{b} = \sum_{i=1}^{n} a_i b_i = a_1 b_1 + a_2 b_2 + \cdots + a_n b_n$$

where Σ denotes summation notation and n is the dimension of the vectors.

a. Matrix determinant lemma   b. Principal axis theorem

c. Conjugate transpose   d. Dot product

27. In mathematics, the term _____ has several different important meanings:

- An _____ is an equality that remains true regardless of the values of any variables that appear within it, to distinguish it from an equality which is true under more particular conditions. For this, the 'triple bar' symbol ≡ is sometimes used.
- In algebra, an _____ or _____ element of a set S with a binary operation Â· is an element e that, when combined with any element x of S, produces that same x. That is, eÂ·x = xÂ·e = x for all x in S.
  - The _____ function from a set S to itself, often denoted id or id_S, s the function such that i = x for all x in S. This function serves as the _____ element in the set of all functions from S to itself with respect to function composition.
  - In linear algebra, the _____ matrix of size n is the n-by-n square matrix with ones on the main diagonal and zeros elsewhere. This matrix serves as the _____ with respect to matrix multiplication.

A common example of the first meaning is the trigonometric _____

$$\sin^2 \theta + \cos^2 \theta = 1$$

which is true for all real values of θ, as opposed to

$$\cos \theta = 1,$$

which is true only for some values of θ, not all. For example, the latter equation is true when $\theta = 0$, false when $\theta = 2$

The concepts of 'additive _____' and 'multiplicative _____' are central to the Peano axioms. The number 0 is the 'additive _____' for integers, real numbers, and complex numbers. For the real numbers, for all $a \in \mathbb{R}$,

$$0 + a = a,$$

$$a + 0 = a, \text{ and}$$

$$0 + 0 = 0.$$

Similarly, The number 1 is the 'multiplicative _____' for integers, real numbers, and complex numbers.

a. Intersection   b. ARIA
c. Action   d. Identity

28. In mathematics, the _____ of a number n is the number that, when added to n, yields zero. The _____ of n is
denoted −n. For example, 7 is −7, because 7 + (−7) = 0, and the _____ of −0.3 is 0.3, because −0.3 + 0.3 = 0.
   a. Algebraic structure   b. Arity
   c. Additive inverse   d. Associativity

29. If A_1, A_2, ..., A_n are _____ square matrices over a field, then

$$\left(A_1 A_2 \cdots A_n\right)^{-1} = A_n^{-1} A_{n-1}^{-1} \cdots A_1^{-1}.$$

It becomes evident why this is the case if one attempts to find an inverse for the product of the A_is from first principles, that is,
that we wish to determine B such that

$$\left(A_1 A_2 \cdots A_n\right)B = I$$

where B is the inverse matrix of the product. To remove A_1 from the product, we can then write

$$A_1^{-1}\left(A_1 A_2 \cdots A_n\right)B = A_1^{-1}I$$

which would reduce the equation to

$$\left(A_2 A_3 \cdots A_n\right)B = A_1^{-1}I.$$

Likewise, then, from

$$A_2^{-1}\left(A_2 A_3 \cdots A_n\right)B = A_2^{-1} A_1^{-1}I$$

which simplifies to

$$\left(A_3 A_4 \cdots A_n\right)B = A_2^{-1} A_1^{-1}I.$$

If one repeat the process up to A_n, the equation becomes

$$\mathbf{B} = \mathbf{A}_n^{-1}\mathbf{A}_{n-1}^{-1}\cdots\mathbf{A}_2^{-1}\mathbf{A}_1^{-1}\mathbf{I}$$

$$\mathbf{B} = \mathbf{A}_n^{-1}\mathbf{A}_{n-1}^{-1}\cdots\mathbf{A}_2^{-1}\mathbf{A}_1^{-1}$$

but B is the inverse matrix, i.e. $\mathbf{B} = \left(\mathbf{A}_1\mathbf{A}_2\cdots\mathbf{A}_n\right)^{-1}$ so the property is established.

Over the field of real numbers, the set of singular n-by-n matrices, considered as a subset of $R^{n\times n}$, is a null set, i.e., has Lebesgue measure zero.

a. Projection-valued measure   b. Matrix pencil

c. Nonsingular   d. Jordan normal form

30. In linear algebra, a _____ is a set of vectors that, in a linear combination, can represent every vector in a given vector space or free module, and such that no element of the set can be represented as a linear combination of the others. In other words, a _____ is a linearly independent spanning set. This picture illustrates the standard _____ in R^2.

a. Chiral   b. Conchoid

c. Basis   d. Dot plot

31. In combinatorial mathematics, a _____ is an un-ordered collection of distinct elements, usually of a prescribed size and taken from a given set. Given such a set S, a _____ of elements of S is just a subset of S, where as always forsets the order of the elements is not taken into account. Also, as always forsets, no elements can be repeated more than once in a _____; this is often referred to as a 'collection without repetition'.

a. Heawood number   b. Sparsity

c. Fill-in   d. Combination

32. In mathematics, _____ are a concept central to linear algebra and related fields of mathematics

Suppose that K is a field and V is a vector space over K.

a. Linear span   b. Linear combinations

c. Setoid   d. Polarization

33. In linear algebra, a family of vectors is _____ if none of them can be written as a linear combination of finitely many other vectors in the collection. A family of vectors which is not _____ is called linearly dependent. For instance, in the three-dimensional real vector space R^3 we have the following example.

a. Direct product   b. Binary function

c. Linear combinations   d. Linearly independent

34. In geometry and trigonometry, an _____ is the figure formed by two rays sharing a common endpoint, called the vertex of the _____. The magnitude of the _____ is the 'amount of rotation' that separates the two rays, and can be measured by considering the length of circular arc swept out when one ray is rotated about the vertex to coincide with the other. Where there is no possibility of confusion, the term '_____' is used interchangeably for both the geometric configuration itself and for its angular magnitude.

a. A posteriori
b. A Mathematical Theory of Communication
c. A chemical equation
d. Angle

35. In mathematics, two vectors are _____ if they are perpendicular. For example, a subway and the street above, although they do not physically intersect, are _____ if they cross at a right angle.

a. Algebraic structure
b. Orthogonal
c. Unique factorization domain
d. Additive identity

36. In mathematics, _____ is one of the basic operations defining a vector space in linear algebra. Note that _____ is different from scalar product which is an inner product between two vectors.

More specifically, if K is a field and V is a vector space over K, then _____ is a function from K × V to V.

a. Scalar multiplication
b. Non-negative matrix factorization
c. Frobenius normal form
d. Jordan normal form

37. In mathematics, an _____ is a vector space with the additional structure of inner product. This additional structure associates each pair of vectors in the space with a scalar quantity known as the inner product of the vectors. Inner products allow the rigorous introduction of intuitive geometrical notions such as the length of a vector or the angle between two vectors.

a. A Mathematical Theory of Communication
b. A chemical equation
c. A posteriori
d. Inner product space

38. In linear algebra, two vectors in an inner product space are _____ if they are orthogonal and both of unit length. A set of vectors form an _____ set if all vectors in the set are mutually orthogonal and all of unit length. An _____ set which forms a basis is called an _____ basis.

a. Orthogonal complement
b. Orthogonalization
c. Orthogonal Procrustes problem
d. Orthonormal

39. In linear algebra, functional analysis and related areas of mathematics, a _____ is a function that assigns a strictly positive length or size to all vectors in a vector space, other than the zero vector. A seminorm, on the other hand, is allowed to assign zero length to some non-zero vectors.

A simple example is the 2-dimensional Euclidean space R^2 equipped with the Euclidean _____.

a. Compression
b. Leibniz formula
c. Going up
d. Norm

40.   In mathematics, an _____ is a statement about the relative size or order of two objects, or about whether they are the same or not

- The notation a < b means that a is less than b.
- The notation a > b means that a is greater than b.
- The notation a ≠ b means that a is not equal to b, but does not say that one is bigger than the other or even that they can be compared in size.

In all these cases, a is not equal to b, hence, '_____'.

These relations are known as strict _____

- The notation a ≤ b means that a is less than or equal to b;
- The notation a ≥ b means that a is greater than or equal to b;

An additional use of the notation is to show that one quantity is much greater than another, normally by several orders of magnitude.

- The notation a << b means that a is much less than b.
- The notation a >> b means that a is much greater than b.

If the sense of the _____ is the same for all values of the variables for which its members are defined, then the _____ is called an 'absolute' or 'unconditional' _____. If the sense of an _____ holds only for certain values of the variables involved, but is reversed or destroyed for other values of the variables, it is called a conditional _____.

An _____ may appear unsolvable because it only states whether a number is larger or smaller than another number; but it is possible to apply the same operations for equalities to inequalities. For example, to find x for the _____ 10x > 23 one would divide 23 by 10.

a. A chemical equation
c. A posteriori

b. Inequality
d. A Mathematical Theory of Communication

41.   In mathematics, specifically in combinatorial commutative algebra, a convex lattice polytope P is called _____ if it has the following property: given any positive integer n, every lattice point of the dilation nP, obtained from P by scaling its vertices by the factor n and taking the convex hull of the resulting points, can be written as the sum of exactly n lattice points in P. This property plays an important role in the theory of toric varieties, where it corresponds to projective normality of the toric variety determined by P.

The simplex in R^k with the vertices at the origin and along the unit coordinate vectors is _____.

a. Polytetrahedron
c. Demihypercubes

b. Hypercube
d. Normal

42.   A justification for choosing this criterion is given in properties below. This minimization problem has a unique solution, provided that the n columns of the matrix X are linearly independent, given by solving the _____

$$(X^\top X)\hat{\boldsymbol{\beta}} = X^\top \mathbf{y}.$$

The primary application of linear least squares is in data fitting. Given a set of m data points $y_1, y_2, \ldots, y_m$, consisting of experimentally measured values taken at m values $x_1, x_2, \ldots, x_m$ of an independent variable (x_i may be scalar or vector quantities), and given a model function $y = f(x, \boldsymbol{\beta})$, with $\boldsymbol{\beta} = (\beta_1, \beta_2, \ldots, \beta_n)$, it is desired to find the parameters β_j such that the model function fits 'best' the data.

a. Constraint optimization   b. Shekel function

c. Slack variable   d. Normal equations

43.   In mathematics, given a linear transformation, an _____ of that linear transformation is a nonzero vector which, when that transformation is applied to it, may change in length, but not direction.

For each _____ of a linear transformation, there is a corresponding scalar value called an eigenvalue for that vector, which determines the amount the _____ is scaled under the linear transformation. For example, an eigenvalue of +2 means that the _____ is doubled in length and points in the same direction.

a. Eigenvector   b. Uncertainty principle

c. Angular momentum   d. Ensemble

44.   In algebra, a _____ is a function depending on n that associates a scalar, de, to every n×n square matrix A. The fundamental geometric meaning of a _____ is as the scale factor for measure when A is regarded as a linear transformation. _____s are important both in calculus, where they enter the substitution rule for several variables, and in multilinear algebra.

a. Pfaffian   b. 1-center problem

c. Functional determinant   d. Determinant

45.   In linear algebra, the _____ of a matrix A is another matrix $A^\top$ created by any one of the following equivalent actions:

- write the rows of A as the columns of $A^\top$
- write the columns of A as the rows of $A^\top$
- reflect A by its main diagonal to obtain $A^\top$

Formally, the _____ of an m × n matrix A is the n × m matrix

$$\mathbf{A}^{\mathrm{T}}_{ij} = \mathbf{A}_{ji} \text{ for } 1 \le i \le n, 1 \le j \le m.$$

- $$\begin{bmatrix} 1 & 2 \\ 3 & 4 \end{bmatrix}^{\mathrm{T}} = \begin{bmatrix} 1 & 3 \\ 2 & 4 \end{bmatrix}.$$

- $$\begin{bmatrix} 1 & 2 \\ 3 & 4 \\ 5 & 6 \end{bmatrix}^{\mathrm{T}} = \begin{bmatrix} 1 & 3 & 5 \\ 2 & 4 & 6 \end{bmatrix}.$$

For matrices A, B and scalar c we have the following properties of _____:

1. $$\left(\mathbf{A}^{\mathrm{T}}\right)^{\mathrm{T}} = \mathbf{A}$$

   Taking the _____ is an involution.

- $$(\mathbf{A} + \mathbf{B})^{\mathrm{T}} = \mathbf{A}^{\mathrm{T}} + \mathbf{B}^{\mathrm{T}}$$

   The _____ respects addition.

- $$(\mathbf{AB})^{\mathrm{T}} = \mathbf{B}^{\mathrm{T}}\mathbf{A}^{\mathrm{T}}$$

   Note that the order of the factors reverses. From this one can deduce that a square matrix A is invertible if and only if A^{T} is invertible, and in this case we have$^{\mathrm{T}} =^{-1}$. It is relatively easy to extend this result to the general case of multiple matrices, where we find that$^{\mathrm{T}} = Z^{\mathrm{T}}Y^{\mathrm{T}}X^{\mathrm{T}}...C^{\mathrm{T}}B^{\mathrm{T}}A^{\mathrm{T}}$.

- $$(c\mathbf{A})^{\mathrm{T}} = c\mathbf{A}^{\mathrm{T}}$$

   The _____ of a scalar is the same scalar. Together with, this states that the _____ is a linear map from the space of m × n matrices to the space of all n × m matrices.

- $$\det(\mathbf{A}^{\mathrm{T}}) = \det(\mathbf{A})$$

The determinant of a matrix is the same as that of its _____.

- The dot product of two column vectors a and b can be computed as

$$\mathbf{a} \cdot \mathbf{b} = \mathbf{a}^{\mathrm{T}}\mathbf{b},$$

which is written as $a_i\, b^i$ in Einstein notation.

- If A has only real entries, then $A^{\mathrm{T}}A$ is a positive-semidefinite matrix.

- $\left(\mathbf{A}^{\mathrm{T}}\right)^{-1} = \left(\mathbf{A}^{-1}\right)^{\mathrm{T}}$

The _____ of an invertible matrix is also invertible, and its inverse is the _____ of the inverse of the original matrix.

- If A is a square matrix, then its eigenvalues are equal to the eigenvalues of its _____.

A square matrix whose _____ is equal to itself is called a symmetric matrix; that is, A is symmetric if

$$\mathbf{A}^{\mathrm{T}} = \mathbf{A}.$$

A square matrix whose _____ is also its inverse is called an orthogonal matrix; that is, G is orthogonal if

$$\mathbf{G}\mathbf{G}^{\mathrm{T}} = \mathbf{G}^{\mathrm{T}}\mathbf{G} = \mathbf{I}_n \text{, the identity matrix.}$$

A square matrix whose _____ is equal to its negative is called skew-symmetric matrix; that is, A is skew-symmetric if

$$\mathbf{A}^{\mathrm{T}} = -\mathbf{A}.$$

The conjugate _____ of the complex matrix A, written as A^{*}, is obtained by taking the _____ of A and the complex conjugate of each entry:

$$\mathbf{A}^{*} = \left(\overline{\mathbf{A}}\right)^{\mathrm{T}} = \overline{\left(\mathbf{A}^{\mathrm{T}}\right)}.$$

If f: V→W is a linear map between vector spaces V and W with nondegenerate bilinear forms, we define the _____ of f to be the linear map $^{t}f : W{\to}V$, determined by

$$B_V(v, {}^{t}f(w)) = B_W(f(v), w) \quad \forall\, v \in V, w \in W.$$

Here, B_V and B_W are the bilinear forms on V and W respectively. The matrix of the _____ of a map is the transposed matrix only if the bases are orthonormal with respect to their bilinear forms.

Over a complex vector space, one often works with sesquilinear forms instead of bilinear.

a. Tridiagonal matrix
c. Transpose

b. Cartan matrix
d. Polynomial matrix

46. _____ generally conveys two primary meanings. The first is an imprecise sense of harmonious or aesthetically-pleasing proportionality and balance; such that it reflects beauty or perfection. The second meaning is a precise and well-defined concept of balance or 'patterned self-similarity' that can be demonstrated or proved according to the rules of a formal system: by geometry, through physics or otherwise.

a. Symmetry
c. Tessellation

b. Symmetry breaking
d. Molecular symmetry

47. In mathematics, a _____ decomposes a periodic function into a sum of simple oscillating functions, namely sines and cosines. The study of _____ is a branch of Fourier analysis. _____ were introduced by Joseph Fourier for the purpose of solving the heat equation in a metal plate.

a. Fourier series of a periodic function converges
c. Fourier series

b. 1-center problem
d. Triangle wave

48. In mathematics, an _____ or member of a set is any one of the distinct objects that make up that set.

Writing A = {1,2,3,4}, means that the _____s of the set A are the numbers 1, 2, 3 and 4. Groups of _____s of A, for example {1,2}, are subsets of A.

a. Universal code
c. Ideal

b. Order
d. Element

49. The _____ is a numerical technique for finding approximate solutions of partial differential equations as well as of integral equations. The solution approach is based either on eliminating the differential equation completely, or rendering the PDE into an approximating system of ordinary differential equations, which are then numerically integrated using standard techniques such as Euler's method, Runge-Kutta, etc.

In solving partial differential equations, the primary challenge is to create an equation that approximates the equation to be studied, but is numerically stable, meaning that errors in the input data and intermediate calculations do not accumulate and cause the resulting output to be meaningless.

a. Spring constant
c. Linear elasticity

b. Fluid flow
d. Finite element method

50. In mathematics, a _____ is often represented as the sum of a sequence of terms. That is, a _____ is represented as a list of numbers with addition operations between them, for example this arithmetic sequence:

1 + 2 + 3 + 4 + 5 + ... + 99 + 100

In most cases of interest the terms of the sequence are produced according to a certain rule, such as by a formula, by an algorithm, by a sequence of measurements, or even by a random number generator.

a. Blind

b. Concavity

c. Contact

d. Series

1. Initial objects are also called _____, and terminal objects are also called final.
    a. Coterminal   b. Terminal object
    c. Colimit   d. Direct limit

2. In mathematics, the _____ of a ring R, often denoted cha, is defined to be the smallest number of times one must add the ring's multiplicative identity element to itself to get the additive identity element; the ring is said to have _____ zero if this repeated sum never reaches the additive identity. That is, cha is the smallest positive number n such that

$$\underbrace{1 + \cdots + 1}_{n \text{ summands}} = 0$$

if such a number n exists, and 0 otherwise. The _____ may also be taken to be the exponent of the ring's additive group, that is, the smallest positive n such that

$$\underbrace{a + \cdots + a}_{n \text{ summands}} = 0$$

for every element a of the ring.

    a. Disk   b. Coherent
    c. Class   d. Characteristic

3. In linear algebra, one associates a polynomial to every square matrix, its _____. This polynomial encodes several important properties of the matrix, most notably its eigenvalues, its determinant and its trace.

    Given a square matrix A, we want to find a polynomial whose roots are precisely the eigenvalues of A.

    a. Characteristic polynomial   b. Coefficient
    c. Littlewood polynomial   d. Polynomial long division

4. In mathematics, a _____ is a constant multiplicative factor of a certain object. For example, in the expression $9x^2$, the _____ of x^2 is 9.

    The object can be such things as a variable, a vector, a function, etc.

    a. Fibonacci polynomials   b. Stability radius
    c. Coefficient   d. Multivariate division algorithm

5. In mathematics, _____s is a term applied to differential operators, and also some difference operators, to signify that they contain no functions of the independent variables, other than constant functions. In other words, it singles out special operators, within the larger class of operators having variable coefficients. Such _____ operators have been found to be the easiest to handle, in several respects.
    a. Peetre theorem   b. Constant coefficient
    c. Semi-elliptic operator   d. Laplace-Beltrami operator

6.   In mathematics, a _____ is an expression constructed from variables and constants, using the operations of addition, subtraction, multiplication, and constant non-negative whole number exponents. For example, $x^2 - 4x + 7$ is a _____, but $x^2 - 4/x + 7x^{3/2}$ is not, because its second term involves division by the variable x and also because its third term contains an exponent that is not a whole number.

_____s are one of the most important concepts in algebra and throughout mathematics and science.

   a. Group extension   b. Polynomial
   c. Semifield   d. Coimage

7.   In vascular plants, the _____ is the organ of a plant body that typically lies below the surface of the soil. This is not always the case, however, since a _____ can also be aerial (that is, growing above the ground) or aerating (that is, growing up above the ground or especially above water.) Furthermore, a stem normally occurring below ground is not exceptional either
   a. 1-center problem   b. 120-cell
   c. 2-3 heap   d. Root

8.   _____ is a phenomenon which arises in the region of a continuous phase transition. Originally reported by Thomas Andrews in 1869 for the liquid-gas transition in carbon dioxide, many other examples have been discovered since. The phenomenon is most commonly demonstrated in binary fluid mixtures, such as methanol and cyclohexane.
   a. Critical opalescence   b. Fermi point
   c. Critical temperature   d. Percolation threshold

9.   In mathematics and in the sciences, a _____ (plural: _____e, formulæ or _____s) is a concise way of expressing information symbolically (as in a mathematical or chemical _____), or a general relationship between quantities. One of many famous _____e is Albert Einstein's $E = mc^2$ (see special relativity

In mathematics, a _____ is a key to solve an equation with variables. For example, the problem of determining the volume of a sphere is one that requires a significant amount of integral calculus to solve.

   a. 1-center problem   b. 120-cell
   c. 2-3 heap   d. Formula

10.   In mathematics, a _____ is a vector space of functions equipped with a norm that is a combination of L^p norms of the function itself as well as its derivatives up to a given order. The derivatives are understood in a suitable weak sense to make the space complete, thus a Banach space. Intuitively, a _____ is a Banach space or Hilbert space of functions with sufficiently many derivatives for some application domain, such as partial differential equations, and equipped with a norm that measures both the size and smoothness of a function.
   a. 2-3 heap   b. 1-center problem
   c. 120-cell   d. Sobolev space

11.   In mathematics, an _____ is a function that is chosen to facilitate the solving of a given ordinary differential equation.

Consider an ordinary differential equation of the form

$$y' + a(x)y = b(x) \qquad (1)$$

where y = y is an unknown function of x, and a and b are given functions.

The _____ method works by turning the left hand side into the form of the derivative of a product.

    a. A Mathematical Theory of Communication   b. Integrating factor

    c. A posteriori   d. A chemical equation

12.   In mathematics, _____ also known as variation of constants, is a general method to solve inhomogeneous linear ordinary differential equations. It was developed by the Italian-French mathematician Joseph Louis Lagrange with noteworthy help from the American mathematician and physicist Noah LaMoyne.

For first-order inhomogeneous linear differential equations it's usually possible to find solutions via integrating factors or undetermined coefficients with considerably less effort, although those methods are rather heuristics that involve guessing and don't work for all inhomogenous linear differential equations.

    a. 120-cell   b. 1-center problem

    c. 2-3 heap   d. Variation of parameters

13.   In mathematics, the _____, name after Ivar Fredholm, is one of Fredholm's theorems and is a result in Fredholm theory. It may be expressed in several ways, as a theorem of linear algebra, a theorem of integral equations, or as a theorem on Fredholm operators. Part of the result states that, a non-zero complex number in the spectrum of a compact operator is an eigenvalue.

    a. Liouville-Neumann series   b. Fredholm integral equation

    c. Fredholm operator   d. Fredholm alternative

14.   _____ is a branch of mathematics that includes the study of limits, derivatives, integrals, and infinite series, and constitutes a major part of modern university education. Historically, it has been referred to as 'the _____ of infinitesimals', or 'infinitesimal _____'. Most basically, _____ is the study of change, in the same way that geometry is the study of space.

    a. Hyperbolic angle   b. Partial sum

    c. Test for Divergence   d. Calculus

15.   The mathematical concept of a _____ expresses the intuitive idea of deterministic dependence between two quantities, one of which is viewed as primary and the other as secondary. A _____ then is a way to associate a unique output for each input of a specified type, for example, a real number or an element of a given set.

    a. Going up   b. Coherent

    c. Grill   d. Function

16.   The _____ specifies the relationship between the two central operations of calculus, differentiation and integration.

The first part of the theorem, sometimes called the first _____, shows that an indefinite integration can be reversed by a differentiation.

The second part, sometimes called the second _____, allows one to compute the definite integral of a function by using any one of its infinitely many antiderivatives.

   a. Maxima and minima
   c. Standard part function

   b. Hyperbolic angle
   d. Fundamental theorem of calculus

17.   In mathematics, a _____ is a statement that can be proved on the basis of explicitly stated or previously agreed assumptions.
   a. Disjunction introduction
   c. Logical value

   b. Boolean function
   d. Theorem

18.   In computational complexity theory, an algorithm is said to take _____ if the asymptotic upper bound for the time it requires is proportional to the size of the input, which is usually denoted n.

Informally spoken, the running time increases linearly with the size of the input. For example, a procedure that adds up all elements of a list requires time proportional to the length of the list.

   a. Time-constructible function
   c. Truth table reduction

   b. Constructible function
   d. Linear time

19.   In mathematics, the _____ or Pythagoras' theorem is a relation in Euclidean geometry among the three sides of a right triangle. The theorem is named after the Greek mathematician Pythagoras, who by tradition is credited with its discovery and proof, although it is often argued that knowledge of the theory predates him.. The theorem is as follows:

In any right triangle, the area of the square whose side is the hypotenuse is equal to the sum of the areas of the squares whose sides are the two legs.

   a. 1-center problem
   c. 2-3 heap

   b. Pythagorean theorem
   d. 120-cell

20.   In ecology, _____ describes a biological interaction where a predator (an organism that is hunting) feeds on its prey, the organism that is attacked. Predators may or may not kill their prey prior to feeding on them, but the act of _____ always results in the death of the prey. The other main category of consumption is detritivory, the consumption of dead organic material (detritus.)
   a. Predator
   c. 1-center problem

   b. 120-cell
   d. Predation

21.   _____ is the right to self-government. _____ is a concept found in moral, political, and bioethical philosophy. Within these contexts, it refers to the capacity of a rational individual to make an informed, un-coerced decision.
   a. Autonomy
   c. A Mathematical Theory of Communication

   b. A posteriori
   d. A chemical equation

22. The requirement that L have strictly positive diagonal entries can be dropped to extend the factorization to the positive semidefinite case. The statement then reads: a square matrix A has a Cholesky decomposition if and only if A is Hermitian and positive semi-definite. _____ for positive semidefinite matrices are not unique in general.
    a. Wold decomposition
    b. Positive definite kernel
    c. Singular values
    d. Cholesky factorizations

23. In general, an object is complete if nothing needs to be added to it. This notion is made more specific in various fields.

In logic, semantic _____ is the converse of soundness for formal systems.

    a. Giuseppe Peano
    b. Logical equality
    c. Set theory
    d. Completeness

24. In probability theory and statistics, the _____ of a family of probability distributions is an important property which basically states that if one has a number of random variates that are 'in the family', any linear combination of these variates will also be 'in the family'. Specifically, the family of probability distributions here is a location-scale family, consisting of probability distributions that differ only in location and scale and 'in the family' means that the random variates have a distribution function that is a member of the family.

The importance of a stable family of probability distributions is that they serve as 'attractors' for linear combinations of non-stable random variates.

    a. Stability
    b. Secant
    c. Torsion
    d. Convergent

25. Suppose that φ : M → N is a smooth map between smooth manifolds; then the _____ of φ at a point x is, in some sense, the best linear approximation of φ near x. It can be viewed as generalization of the total derivative of ordinary calculus. Explicitly, it is a linear map from the tangent space of M at x to the tangent space of N at φ
    a. Concurrent
    b. Grill
    c. Boundary
    d. Differential

26. _____s arise in many problems in physics, engineering, etc. The following examples show how to solve _____s in a few simple cases when an exact solution exists.

A separable linear ordinary _____ of the first order has the general form:

$$\frac{dy}{dt} + f(t)y = 0$$

where f is some known function.

    a. Differential equation
    b. Nahm equations
    c. Nullcline
    d. Homogeneous differential equation

27. _____ is a differential equation for which certain numerical methods for solving the equation are numerically unstable, unless the step size is taken to be extremely small.
   a. Stiff differential equation
   b. 120-cell
   c. 2-3 heap
   d. 1-center problem

28. In mathematics and computational science, the _____, named after Leonhard Euler, is a first order numerical procedure for solving ordinary differential equations with a given initial value. It is the most basic kind of explicit method for numerical integration for ordinary differential equations.

Consider the problem of calculating the shape of an unknown curve which starts at a given point and satisfies a given differential equation.

   a. Uniform theory of diffraction
   b. Analytic element method
   c. Explicit and implicit methods
   d. Euler method

29. In applied mathematics, explicit and implicit methods are approaches used in computer simulations of physical processes they are numerical methods for solving time-variable ordinary and partial differential equations.

_____s calculate the state of a system at a later time from the state of the system at the current time, while an implicit method finds it by solving an equation involving both the current state of the system and the later one.

   a. Analytic element method
   b. Explicit and implicit methods
   c. Explicit method
   d. Uniform theory of diffraction

30. In applied mathematics, explicit and _____s are approaches used in computer simulations of physical processes they are numerical methods for solving time-variable ordinary and partial differential equations.

Explicit methods calculate the state of a system at a later time from the state of the system at the current time, while an _____ finds it by solving an equation involving both the current state of the system and the later one. Mathematically, if Y is the current system state and Y is the state at the later time, then, for an explicit method

$$Y(t + \Delta t) = F(Y(t))$$

while for an _____ one solves an equation

$$G(Y(t), Y(t + \Delta t)) = 0 \qquad (1)$$

to find Y

It is clear that _____s require an extra computation, and they can be much harder to implement.

a. Euler-Maruyama method   b. Explicit method
c. Explicit and implicit methods   d. Implicit method

31. The _____ or Dirac's delta is a mathematical construct introduced by the British theoretical physicist Paul Dirac. Informally, it is a function representing an infinitely sharp peak bounding unit area: a function that has the value zero everywhere except at x = 0 where its value is infinitely large in such a way that its total integral is 1. It is a continuous analogue of the discrete Kronecker delta.

a. Schwartz kernel theorem   b. Weak derivative
c. Hyperfunction   d. Dirac delta

32. In linear algebra, _____ is an efficient algorithm for solving systems of linear equations, finding the rank of a matrix, and calculating the inverse of an invertible square matrix. _____ is named after German mathematician and scientist Carl Friedrich Gauss.

Elementary row operations are used to reduce a matrix to row echelon form.

a. Crout matrix decomposition   b. Conjugate gradient method
c. Cholesky decomposition   d. Gaussian elimination

33. In mathematics, _____ are objects generalizing the notion of functions. There is more than one recognised theory. _____ are especially useful in making discontinuous functions more like smooth functions, and (going to extremes) describing physical phenomena such as point charges.

a. Logarithmically-spaced Dirac comb   b. Weak derivative
c. Generalized functions   d. Test function

34. A _____ is a single identifiable localized source of something. A _____ has negligible extent, distinguishing it from other source geometries. Sources are called _____s because in mathematical modeling, these sources can usually be approximated as a mathematical point to simplify analysis.

a. 120-cell   b. 2-3 heap
c. 1-center problem   d. Point source

35. The Dirac delta or Dirac's delta is a mathematical construct introduced by theoretical physicist Paul Dirac. Informally, it is a function representing an infinitely sharp peak bounding unit area: a function $\delta(x)$ that has the value zero everywhere except at x = 0 where its value is infinitely large in such a way that its total integral is 1. In the context of signal processing it is often referred to as the _____ function.

a. A posteriori   b. A chemical equation
c. A Mathematical Theory of Communication   d. Unit impulse

1. In mathematics, a _____ is a vector space of functions equipped with a norm that is a combination of L^P norms of the function itself as well as its derivatives up to a given order. The derivatives are understood in a suitable weak sense to make the space complete, thus a Banach space. Intuitively, a _____ is a Banach space or Hilbert space of functions with sufficiently many derivatives for some application domain, such as partial differential equations, and equipped with a norm that measures both the size and smoothness of a function.

   a. 2-3 heap
   b. 1-center problem
   c. 120-cell
   d. Sobolev space

2. In abstract algebra, a field extension L /K is called _____ if every element of L is _____ over K. Field extensions which are not _____.

For example, the field extension R/Q, that is the field of real numbers as an extension of the field of rational numbers, is transcendental, while the field extensions C/R and Q

   a. Identity
   b. Echo
   c. Ideal
   d. Algebraic

3. In commutative algebra, the notions of an element _____ over a ring, and of an _____ extension of rings, are a generalization of the notions in field theory of an element being algebraic over a field, and of an algebraic extension of fields.

The special case of greatest interest in number theory is that of complex numbers _____ over the ring of integers Z.

The term ring will be understood to mean commutative ring with a unit.

   a. Arc length
   b. Integral test for convergence
   c. Antidifferentiation
   d. Integral

4. A _____ is a mathematical model of a system based on the use of a linear operator. _____s typically exhibit features and properties that are much simpler than the general, nonlinear case. As a mathematical abstraction or idealization, _____s find important applications in automatic control theory, signal processing, and telecommunications.

   a. Predispositioning Theory
   b. Hybrid system
   c. Percolation
   d. Linear system

5. In mathematics, a _____ is a rectangular table of elements, which may be numbers or, more generally, any abstract quantities that can be added and multiplied. Matrices are used to describe linear equations, keep track of the coefficients of linear transformations and to record data that depend on multiple parameters. Matrices are described by the field of _____ theory.

   a. Coherent
   b. Compression
   c. Double counting
   d. Matrix

6. Suppose that φ : M → N is a smooth map between smooth manifolds; then the _____ of φ at a point x is, in some sense, the best linear approximation of φ near x. It can be viewed as generalization of the total derivative of ordinary calculus. Explicitly, it is a linear map from the tangent space of M at x to the tangent space of N at φ

a. Grill   b. Boundary

c. Differential   d. Concurrent

7.   The mathematical concept of a _____ expresses the intuitive idea of deterministic dependence between two
quantities, one of which is viewed as primary and the other as secondary. A _____ then is a way to associate a unique
output for each input of a specified type, for example, a real number or an element of a given set.

a. Function   b. Going up

c. Coherent   d. Grill

8.   In mathematics, a linear map is a function between two vector spaces that preserves the operations of vector addition and
scalar multiplication. The expression '_____' is in especially common use, for linear maps from a vector space to itself In
advanced mathematics, the definition of linear function coincides with the definition of linear map.

a. Hubbard-Stratonovich transformation   b. Morphism

c. Morphisms   d. Linear operator

9.   In physics, an _____ is a function acting on the space of physical states. As a result of its application on a physical
state, another physical state is obtained, very often along with some extra relevant information.

The simplest example of the utility of _____s is the study of symmetry.

a. Algebraic signal processing   b. Operand

c. Operator   d. Affine Hecke algebra

10.   In physics and in _____ calculus, a _____ is a concept characterized by a magnitude and a direction. A
_____ can be thought of as an arrow in Euclidean space, drawn from an initial point A pointing to a terminal point B.

a. Dominance   b. Constraint

c. Vector   d. Deviation

11.   In mathematics, a _____ is a collection of objects called vectors that may be scaled and added. These two
operations must adhere to a number of axioms that generalize common properties of tuples of real numbers such as vectors in
the plane or three-dimensional Euclidean space. _____s are a keystone of linear algebra, and much of their theory is of a
linear nature.

a. Vector space   b. Geodesic

c. Moment of inertia   d. Minkowski space

12.   In topology, the _____ of a subset S of a topological space X is the set of points which can be approached both from
S and from the outside of S. More formally, it is the set of points in the closure of S, not belonging to the interior of S. An
element of the _____ of S is called a _____ point of S.

a. Heap   b. Character

c. Bertrand paradox   d. Boundary

13.   In mathematics, in the field of differential equations, a boundary value problem is a differential equation together with a
set of additional restraints, called the _____. A solution to a boundary value problem is a solution to the differential
equation which also satisfies the _____.

Boundary value problems arise in several branches of physics as any physical differential equation will have them.

a. Total differential equation
c. Separation of variables

b. Boundary value problem
d. Boundary conditions

14.   In mathematics, an _____ is a statement about the relative size or order of two objects, or about whether they are the same or not

- The notation a < b means that a is less than b.
- The notation a > b means that a is greater than b.
- The notation a ≠ b means that a is not equal to b, but does not say that one is bigger than the other or even that they can be compared in size.

In all these cases, a is not equal to b, hence, '_____'.

These relations are known as strict _____

- The notation a ≤ b means that a is less than or equal to b;
- The notation a ≥ b means that a is greater than or equal to b;

An additional use of the notation is to show that one quantity is much greater than another, normally by several orders of magnitude.

- The notation a << b means that a is much less than b.
- The notation a >> b means that a is much greater than b.

If the sense of the _____ is the same for all values of the variables for which its members are defined, then the _____ is called an 'absolute' or 'unconditional' _____. If the sense of an _____ holds only for certain values of the variables involved, but is reversed or destroyed for other values of the variables, it is called a conditional _____.

An _____ may appear unsolvable because it only states whether a number is larger or smaller than another number; but it is possible to apply the same operations for equalities to inequalities. For example, to find x for the _____ 10x > 23 one would divide 23 by 10.

a. A chemical equation
c. A posteriori

b. Inequality
d. A Mathematical Theory of Communication

15.   In mathematics, a _____ is an operator defined as a function of the differentiation operator. It is helpful, as a matter of notation first, to consider differentiation as an abstract operation, accepting a function and returning another.

There are certainly reasons not to restrict to linear operators; for instance the Schwarzian derivative is a well-known non-linear operator.

a. Hessian matrix
c. Surface integral

b. Differential operator
d. Symmetry of second derivatives

16. _____ is a core concept of basic mathematics, specifically in the fields of infinitesimal calculus and mathematical analysis. Given a function f

$$\int_a^b f(x)\, dx\,,$$

is equal to the area of a region in the xy-plane bounded by the graph of f, the x-axis, and the vertical lines x = a and x = b, with areas below the x-axis being subtracted.

The term 'integral' may also refer to the notion of antiderivative, a function F whose derivative is the given function f.

a. OMAC   b. Apex
c. Integration   d. Epigraph

17.   In calculus, and more generally in mathematical analysis, _____ is a rule that transforms the integral of products of functions into other, hopefully simpler, integrals. The rule arises from the product rule of differentiation.

If u = f[x], v = g[x], and the differentials du = f '[x] dx and dv = g'[x] dx; then in its simplest form the product rule is:

a. Integration by parts   b. Integral test for convergence
c. Integration by parts operator   d. Arc length

18.   In linear algebra, a _____ is a square matrix, A, that is equal to its transpose

$$A = A^T.$$

The entries of a _____ are symmetric with respect to the main diagonal. So if the entries are written as A =, then

$$a_{ij} = a_{ji}$$

for all indices i and j. The following 3×3 matrix is symmetric:

$$\begin{bmatrix} 1 & 2 & 3 \\ 2 & 4 & -5 \\ 3 & -5 & 6 \end{bmatrix}.$$

A matrix is called skew-symmetric or antisymmetric if its transpose is the same as its negative.

a. Broken-line graph
b. Conway triangle notation
c. Contour integration
d. Symmetric matrix

19.   In mathematics, in the field of differential equations, a _____ is a differential equation together with a set of additional restraints, called the boundary conditions. A solution to a _____ is a solution to the differential equation which also satisfies the boundary conditions.

_____s arise in several branches of physics as any physical differential equation will have them.

a. Riccati equation
b. Separation of variables
c. Boundary value problem
d. Normal mode

20.   The requirement that L have strictly positive diagonal entries can be dropped to extend the factorization to the positive semidefinite case. The statement then reads: a square matrix A has a Cholesky decomposition if and only if A is Hermitian and positive semi-definite. _____ for positive semidefinite matrices are not unique in general.
a. Positive definite kernel
b. Singular values
c. Wold decomposition
d. Cholesky factorizations

21.   In mathematics, a _____ decomposes a periodic function into a sum of simple oscillating functions, namely sines and cosines. The study of _____ is a branch of Fourier analysis. _____ were introduced by Joseph Fourier for the purpose of solving the heat equation in a metal plate.
a. 1-center problem
b. Fourier series of a periodic function converges
c. Triangle wave
d. Fourier series

22.   In mathematics, a _____ is a constant multiplicative factor of a certain object. For example, in the expression $9x^2$, the _____ of x^2 is 9.

The object can be such things as a variable, a vector, a function, etc.

a. Multivariate division algorithm
b. Stability radius
c. Fibonacci polynomials
d. Coefficient

23.   In mathematics, a _____ is often represented as the sum of a sequence of terms. That is, a _____ is represented as a list of numbers with addition operations between them, for example this arithmetic sequence:

   1 + 2 + 3 + 4 + 5 + ... + 99 + 100

In most cases of interest the terms of the sequence are produced according to a certain rule, such as by a formula, by an algorithm, by a sequence of measurements, or even by a random number generator.

a. Blind
b. Series
c. Concavity
d. Contact

24.   The _____ of an angle is the ratio of the length of the opposite side to the length of the hypotenuse. In our case

$$\sin A = \frac{\text{opposite}}{\text{hypotenuse}} = \frac{a}{h}.$$

Note that this ratio does not depend on size of the particular right triangle chosen, as long as it contains the angle A, since all such triangles are similar.

The cosine of an angle is the ratio of the length of the adjacent side to the length of the hypotenuse.

a. Law of sines   b. Trigonometric functions
c. Right angle   d. Sine

25.   In mathematics, the _____ or Pythagoras' theorem is a relation in Euclidean geometry among the three sides of a right triangle. The theorem is named after the Greek mathematician Pythagoras, who by tradition is credited with its discovery and proof, although it is often argued that knowledge of the theory predates him.. The theorem is as follows:

In any right triangle, the area of the square whose side is the hypotenuse is equal to the sum of the areas of the squares whose sides are the two legs.

a. 1-center problem   b. 120-cell
c. 2-3 heap   d. Pythagorean theorem

26.   In mathematics, a _____ is a statement that can be proved on the basis of explicitly stated or previously agreed assumptions.
a. Logical value   b. Boolean function
c. Disjunction introduction   d. Theorem

27.   In mathematics, a topological space X with topology Ω is said to be _____ if

- 1) X is compact and T_0;
- 2) The set C(X) of all relatively compact open subsets of (X,Ω) is a sublattice of Ω and a base for the topology.
- 3) X is sober, that is any nonempty closed set F which is not a closure of a singleton {x} is a union of two closed sets which differ from F.

a. Cocountable topology   b. Hedgehog space
c. Spectral   d. Second-countable space

28.   _____ are a class of techniques used in applied mathematics and scientific computing to numerically solve certain partial differential equations, often involving the use of the Fast Fourier Transform. Where applicable, _____ have excellent error properties, with the so called 'exponential convergence' being the fastest possible.

PDEs describe a wide array of physical processes such as heat conduction, fluid flow, and sound propagation.

a. Numerical continuation

b. Truncated power function

c. Pseudo-spectral methods

d. Spectral methods

29.   In mathematics, an _____ or member of a set is any one of the distinct objects that make up that set.

Writing A = {1,2,3,4}, means that the _____ s of the set A are the numbers 1, 2, 3 and 4. Groups of _____ s of A, for example {1,2}, are subsets of A.

a. Order

b. Ideal

c. Universal code

d. Element

30.   The _____ is a numerical technique for finding approximate solutions of partial differential equations as well as of integral equations. The solution approach is based either on eliminating the differential equation completely, or rendering the PDE into an approximating system of ordinary differential equations, which are then numerically integrated using standard techniques such as Euler's method, Runge-Kutta, etc.

In solving partial differential equations, the primary challenge is to create an equation that approximates the equation to be studied, but is numerically stable, meaning that errors in the input data and intermediate calculations do not accumulate and cause the resulting output to be meaningless.

a. Finite element method

b. Fluid flow

c. Linear elasticity

d. Spring constant

31.   In mathematics, in the area of numerical analysis, _____ are a class of methods for converting a continuous operator problem (such as a differential equation) to a discrete problem. In principle, it is the equivalent of applying the method of variation to a function space, by converting the equation to a weak formulation. Typically one then applies some constraints on the functions space to characterize the space with a finite set of basis functions.

a. Condition number

b. Low-discrepancy sequence

c. Spectral methods

d. Galerkin methods

32.   In physics, the law of _____ states that the total amount of energy in an isolated system remains constant. A consequence of this law is that energy cannot be created or destroyed. The only thing that can happen with energy in an isolated system is that it can change form, that is to say for instance kinetic energy can become thermal energy.

a. 2-3 heap

b. 120-cell

c. 1-center problem

d. Conservation of energy

33.   In signal processing, the _____ E_s of a continuous-time signal x

$$E_s \;=\; \langle x(t), x(t) \rangle \;=\; \int_{-\infty}^{\infty} |x(t)|^2 dt$$

_____ in this context is not, strictly speaking, the same as the conventional notion of _____ in physics and the other sciences. The two concepts are, however, closely related, and it is possible to convert from one to the other:

$$E = \frac{E_s}{Z} = \frac{1}{Z} \int_{-\infty}^{\infty} |x(t)|^2 dt$$

where Z represents the magnitude, in appropriate units of measure, of the load driven by the signal.

For example, if x

a. Emphasis   b. Audio signal processing
c. Essential bandwidth   d. Energy

34.   In mathematics, a _____ is an expression constructed from variables and constants, using the operations of addition, subtraction, multiplication, and constant non-negative whole number exponents. For example, $x^2 - 4x + 7$ is a _____, but $x^2 - 4/x + 7x^{3/2}$ is not, because its second term involves division by the variable x and also because its third term contains an exponent that is not a whole number.

_____s are one of the most important concepts in algebra and throughout mathematics and science.

a. Polynomial   b. Group extension
c. Coimage   d. Semifield

35.

    • _____ difference
    • _____ energy

a. 2-3 heap   b. 120-cell
c. 1-center problem   d. Potential

36.   _____ can be thought of as energy stored within a physical system. It is called _____ because it has the potential to be converted into other forms of energy, such as kinetic energy, and to do work in the process. The standard unit of measure for _____ is the joule, the same as for work, or energy in general.
a. 120-cell   b. 2-3 heap
c. 1-center problem   d. Potential energy

37.   The _____ , is achieved in a packed stadium when successive groups of spectators briefly stand and raise their arms. Each spectator is required to rise at the same time as those straight in front and behind, and slightly after the person immediately to either the right or the left. Immediately upon stretching to full height, the spectator returns to the usual seated position.

a. Pauli exclusion principle

b. Wave

c. Lagrangian

d. Thermodynamic limit

38.   The _____ is an important second-order linear partial differential equation that describes the propagation of a variety of waves, such as sound waves, light waves and water waves. It arises in fields such as acoustics, electromagnetics, and fluid dynamics. Historically, the problem of a vibrating string such as that of a musical instrument was studied by Jean le Rond d'Alembert, Leonhard Euler, Daniel Bernoulli, and Joseph-Louis Lagrange.

a. Random walk

b. Cauchy momentum equation

c. Wave equation

d. Lagrangian

39.   In economics, an externality is an impact on any party not directly involved in an economic decision. An externality occurs when an economic activity causes _____ costs or _____ benefits to third party stakeholders who did not directly affect the economic transaction. Another term that often replaces externality is spillover.

a. External

b. A chemical equation

c. A Mathematical Theory of Communication

d. A posteriori

40.   To define the derivative of a distribution, we first consider the case of a differentiable and integrable function f : R → R. If φ is a _____, then we have

$$\int_{\mathbf{R}} f'\varphi \, dx = - \int_{\mathbf{R}} f\varphi' \, dx$$

using integration by parts (note that φ is zero outside of a bounded set and that therefore no boundary values have to be taken into account.) This suggests that if S is a distribution, we should define its derivative S' by

$$\langle S', \varphi \rangle = - \langle S, \varphi' \rangle.$$

a. Generalized functions

b. Hyperfunction

c. Schwartz kernel theorem

d. Test function

41.   In mathematics, a _____ on a vector space V is a bilinear mapping V × V → F, where F is the field of scalars. That is, a _____ is a function B: V × V → F which is linear in each argument separately:

$$1. \ B(u + u', v) = B(u, v) + B(u', v),$$
$$2. \ B(u, v + v') = B(u, v) + B(u, v'),$$
$$3. \ B(\lambda u, v) = B(u, \lambda v) = \lambda B(u, v).$$

Any _____ on Fⁿ can be expressed as

$$B(\mathbf{x}, \mathbf{y}) = \mathbf{x}^\mathsf{T} A \mathbf{y} = \sum_{i,j=1}^{n} a_{ij} x_i y_j$$

where A is an n × n matrix.

The definition of a _____ can easily be extended to include modules over a commutative ring, with linear maps replaced by module homomorphisms.

a. Degenerate form   b. 120-cell

c. Bilinear form   d. 1-center problem

42.   In mathematics, an _____ is a vector space with the additional structure of inner product. This additional structure associates each pair of vectors in the space with a scalar quantity known as the inner product of the vectors. Inner products allow the rigorous introduction of intuitive geometrical notions such as the length of a vector or the angle between two vectors.

a. A chemical equation   b. A Mathematical Theory of Communication

c. A posteriori   d. Inner product space

43.   In linear algebra, functional analysis and related areas of mathematics, a _____ is a function that assigns a strictly positive length or size to all vectors in a vector space, other than the zero vector. A seminorm, on the other hand, is allowed to assign zero length to some non-zero vectors.

A simple example is the 2-dimensional Euclidean space R^2 equipped with the Euclidean _____.

a. Going up   b. Leibniz formula

c. Compression   d. Norm

44.   In linear algebra and functional analysis, a _____ is a linear transformation P from a vector space to itself such that $P^2 = P$. It leaves its image unchanged. Though abstract, this definition of '_____' formalizes and generalizes the idea of graphical _____.

a. Characteristic function   b. Deviance

c. Critical point   d. Projection

45.   In linear algebra, a _____ is a set of vectors that, in a linear combination, can represent every vector in a given vector space or free module, and such that no element of the set can be represented as a linear combination of the others. In other words, a _____ is a linearly independent spanning set. This picture illustrates the standard _____ in R^2.

a. Chiral   b. Dot plot

c. Conchoid   d. Basis

46.   In mathematics, two vectors are _____ if they are perpendicular. For example, a subway and the street above, although they do not physically intersect, are _____ if they cross at a right angle.

a. Additive identity   b. Algebraic structure

c. Orthogonal   d. Unique factorization domain

47.   Elements in an _____ do not have to be unit vectors, but must be mutually perpendicular. It is easy to change the vectors in an _____ by scalar multiples to get an orthonormal basis, and indeed this is a typical way that an orthonormal basis is constructed.

The standard basis of the n-dimensional Euclidean space R^n is an example of orthonormal (and ordered) basis.

a. A Mathematical Theory of Communication   b. A chemical equation

c. A posteriori   d. Orthogonal basis

48. In topology and related areas of mathematics, a subset A of a topological space X is called _____ if, intuitively, any point in X can be 'well-approximated' by points in A. Formally, A is _____ in X if for any point x in X, any neighborhood of x contains at least one point from A.

Equivalently, A is _____ in X if the only closed subset of X containing A is X itself.

a. Dense

b. Harmonic series

c. Crib

d. Composite

49. In the mathematical subfield of numerical analysis a _____ is a matrix populated primarily with zeros.

Conceptually, sparsity corresponds to systems which are loosely coupled. Consider a line of balls connected by springs from one to the next; this is a sparse system.

a. Pigeonhole principle

b. Macdonald polynomials

c. Binomial coefficient

d. Sparse matrix

50. In cryptography, _____ is a block cipher designed in 2002 by Jorge Nakahara, Jr., Vincent Rijmen, Bart Preneel, and Joos Vandewalle. _____ is based directly on IDEA and uses the same basic operations.

_____ is actually a family of 3 variant ciphers with block sizes of 64, 96, and 128 bits.

a. Key server

b. Mesh

c. Depth

d. Duality

51. In linear algebra, a _____ matrix is a matrix that is 'almost' a diagonal matrix. To be exact: a _____ matrix has nonzero elements only in the main diagonal, the first diagonal below this, and the first diagonal above the main diagonal.

For example, the following matrix is _____:

$$\begin{pmatrix} 1 & 4 & 0 & 0 \\ 3 & 4 & 1 & 0 \\ 0 & 2 & 3 & 4 \\ 0 & 0 & 1 & 3 \end{pmatrix}.$$

A determinant formed from a _____ matrix is known as a continuant.

a. Transition matrix

b. Pascal matrix

c. Random matrix

d. Tridiagonal

52. In linear algebra, a _____ is a matrix that is 'almost' a diagonal matrix. To be exact: a _____ has nonzero elements only in the main diagonal, the first diagonal below this, and the first diagonal above the main diagonal.

For example, the following matrix is tridiagonal:

$$\begin{pmatrix} 1 & 4 & 0 & 0 \\ 3 & 4 & 1 & 0 \\ 0 & 2 & 3 & 4 \\ 0 & 0 & 1 & 3 \end{pmatrix}$$

A determinant formed from a _____ is known as a continuant.

   a. Tridiagonal matrix   b. Stochastic matrix
   c. Sylvester matrix   d. Transition matrix

53.   In mathematics, particularly numerical analysis, a _____ is an element of the basis for a function space. The term is a degeneration of the term basis vector for a more general vector space; that is, each function in the function space can be represented as a linear combination of the _____s.

The collection of quadratic polynomials with real coefficients has $\{1, t, t^2\}$ as a basis.

   a. Basis function   b. Constructions of low-discrepancy sequences
   c. Meshfree methods   d. Bernstein polynomial

54.   In linear algebra, _____ is an efficient algorithm for solving systems of linear equations, finding the rank of a matrix, and calculating the inverse of an invertible square matrix. _____ is named after German mathematician and scientist Carl Friedrich Gauss.

Elementary row operations are used to reduce a matrix to row echelon form.

   a. Crout matrix decomposition   b. Cholesky decomposition
   c. Conjugate gradient method   d. Gaussian elimination

55.   The _____ or Dirac's delta is a mathematical construct introduced by the British theoretical physicist Paul Dirac. Informally, it is a function representing an infinitely sharp peak bounding unit area: a function that has the value zero everywhere except at x = 0 where its value is infinitely large in such a way that its total integral is 1. It is a continuous analogue of the discrete Kronecker delta.
   a. Weak derivative   b. Schwartz kernel theorem
   c. Hyperfunction   d. Dirac delta

56.   In mathematics, _____ are objects generalizing the notion of functions. There is more than one recognised theory. _____ are especially useful in making discontinuous functions more like smooth functions, and (going to extremes) describing physical phenomena such as point charges.
   a. Test function   b. Generalized functions
   c. Weak derivative   d. Logarithmically-spaced Dirac comb

57.   In mathematics, the _____ of a number n is the number that, when added to n, yields zero. The _____ of n is denoted −n. For example, 7 is −7, because 7 + (−7) = 0, and the _____ of −0.3 is 0.3, because −0.3 + 0.3 = 0.

  a. Arity

  c. Algebraic structure

             b. Associativity

             d. Additive inverse

1. In mathematics, a _____ decomposes a periodic function into a sum of simple oscillating functions, namely sines and cosines. The study of _____ is a branch of Fourier analysis. _____ were introduced by Joseph Fourier for the purpose of solving the heat equation in a metal plate.

   a. Fourier series of a periodic function converges
   c. Triangle wave

   b. 1-center problem
   d. Fourier series

2. In mathematics, a _____ is often represented as the sum of a sequence of terms. That is, a _____ is represented as a list of numbers with addition operations between them, for example this arithmetic sequence:

$$1 + 2 + 3 + 4 + 5 + ... + 99 + 100$$

In most cases of interest the terms of the sequence are produced according to a certain rule, such as by a formula, by an algorithm, by a sequence of measurements, or even by a random number generator.

   a. Concavity
   c. Series

   b. Contact
   d. Blind

3. The _____ of an angle is the ratio of the length of the opposite side to the length of the hypotenuse. In our case

$$\sin A = \frac{\text{opposite}}{\text{hypotenuse}} = \frac{a}{h}.$$

Note that this ratio does not depend on size of the particular right triangle chosen, as long as it contains the angle A, since all such triangles are similar.

The cosine of an angle is the ratio of the length of the adjacent side to the length of the hypotenuse.

   a. Sine
   c. Law of sines

   b. Trigonometric functions
   d. Right angle

4. _____ is the partial or full removal of units from a mathematical equation by a suitable substitution of variables. This technique can simplify and parameterize problems where measured units are involved. It is closely related to dimensional analysis.

   a. 1-center problem
   c. 2-3 heap

   b. 120-cell
   d. Nondimensionalization

5. The requirement that L have strictly positive diagonal entries can be dropped to extend the factorization to the positive semidefinite case. The statement then reads: a square matrix A has a Cholesky decomposition if and only if A is Hermitian and positive semi-definite. _____ for positive semidefinite matrices are not unique in general.

   a. Positive definite kernel
   c. Singular values

   b. Wold decomposition
   d. Cholesky factorizations

6. In chemistry, _____ is the measure of how much of a given substance there is mixed with another substance. This can apply to any sort of chemical mixture, but most frequently the concept is limited to homogeneous solutions, where it refers to the amount of solute in the solvent.

To concentrate a solution, one must add more solute, or reduce the amount of solvent (for instance, by selective evaporation.)

a. 1-center problem   b. 120-cell
c. 2-3 heap   d. Concentration

7.   In computational complexity theory, an algorithm is said to take _____ if the asymptotic upper bound for the time it requires is proportional to the size of the input, which is usually denoted n.

Informally spoken, the running time increases linearly with the size of the input. For example, a procedure that adds up all elements of a list requires time proportional to the length of the list.

a. Linear time   b. Time-constructible function
c. Truth table reduction   d. Constructible function

8.   In mathematics, a _____ is a vector space of functions equipped with a norm that is a combination of L^p norms of the function itself as well as its derivatives up to a given order. The derivatives are understood in a suitable weak sense to make the space complete, thus a Banach space. Intuitively, a _____ is a Banach space or Hilbert space of functions with sufficiently many derivatives for some application domain, such as partial differential equations, and equipped with a norm that measures both the size and smoothness of a function.

a. 1-center problem   b. 120-cell
c. 2-3 heap   d. Sobolev space

9.   In mathematics, _____ is any of several methods for solving ordinary and partial differential equations, in which algebra allows one to re-write an equation so that each of two variables occurs on a different side of the equation.

Suppose a differential equation can be written in the form

$$\frac{d}{dx}f(x) = g(x)h(f(x)), \qquad (1)$$

which we can write more simply by letting y = f:

$$\frac{dy}{dx} = g(x)h(y).$$

As long as h≠ 0, we can rearrange terms to obtain:

$$\frac{dy}{h(y)} = g(x)dx,$$

so that the two variables x and y have been separated.

Some who dislike Leibniz's notation may prefer to write this as

$$\frac{1}{h(y)}\frac{dy}{dx} = g(x),$$

but that fails to make it quite as obvious why this is called '_____'.

   a. Wronskian   b. Sturm-Liouville equation
   c. Normal mode   d. Separation of variables

10.   In mathematics and logic, the phrase 'there is one and only one' is used to indicate that exactly one object with a certain property exists. In mathematical logic, this sort of quantification is known as _____ quantification or unique existential quantification.

_____ quantification is often denoted with the symbols '∃!' or $∃_{=1}$'.

   a. A Mathematical Theory of Communication   b. A chemical equation
   c. A posteriori   d. Uniqueness

11.   In mathematics, the _____, name after Ivar Fredholm, is one of Fredholm's theorems and is a result in Fredholm theory. It may be expressed in several ways, as a theorem of linear algebra, a theorem of integral equations, or as a theorem on Fredholm operators. Part of the result states that, a non-zero complex number in the spectrum of a compact operator is an eigenvalue.

   a. Fredholm operator   b. Liouville-Neumann series
   c. Fredholm alternative   d. Fredholm integral equation

12.   In mathematics, the _____s are analogs of the ordinary trigonometric functions. The basic _____s are the hyperbolic sine 'sinh', and the hyperbolic cosine 'cosh', from which are derived the hyperbolic tangent 'tanh', etc., in analogy to the derived trigonometric functions. The inverse _____ are the area hyperbolic sine 'arsinh' (also called 'asinh', or sometimes by the misnomer of 'arcsinh') and so on.

   a. Square root   b. Rectangular function
   c. Heaviside step function   d. Hyperbolic function

13.   The _____ is an important partial differential equation which describes the distribution of heat in a given region over time. For a function u

$$\frac{\partial u}{\partial t} - k\left(\frac{\partial^2 u}{\partial x^2} + \frac{\partial^2 u}{\partial y^2} + \frac{\partial^2 u}{\partial z^2}\right) = 0$$

where k is a constant.

The _____ is of fundamental importance in diverse scientific fields.

a. 1-center problem

b. 120-cell

c. 2-3 heap

d. Heat equation

14. Initial objects are also called _____, and terminal objects are also called final.

a. Direct limit

b. Coterminal

c. Colimit

d. Terminal object

15. In topology, the _____ of a subset S of a topological space X is the set of points which can be approached both from S and from the outside of S. More formally, it is the set of points in the closure of S, not belonging to the interior of S. An element of the _____ of S is called a _____ point of S.

a. Bertrand paradox

b. Heap

c. Character

d. Boundary

16. In mathematics, in the field of differential equations, a boundary value problem is a differential equation together with a set of additional restraints, called the _____. A solution to a boundary value problem is a solution to the differential equation which also satisfies the _____.

Boundary value problems arise in several branches of physics as any physical differential equation will have them.

a. Boundary value problem

b. Total differential equation

c. Separation of variables

d. Boundary conditions

17. In differential geometry there are a number of second-order, linear, elliptic differential operators bearing the name _____

The connection _____ is a differential operator acting on the various tensor bundles of a manifold, defined in terms of a Riemmanian- or pseudo-Riemannian metric.

a. Multivariable calculus

b. Shift theorem

c. Laplacian

d. Differential operator

18. In linear algebra, a _____ is a set of vectors that, in a linear combination, can represent every vector in a given vector space or free module, and such that no element of the set can be represented as a linear combination of the others. In other words, a _____ is a linearly independent spanning set. This picture illustrates the standard _____ in R^2.

a. Dot plot

b. Conchoid

c. Chiral

d. Basis

19. In mathematics, particularly numerical analysis, a _____ is an element of the basis for a function space. The term is a degeneration of the term basis vector for a more general vector space; that is, each function in the function space can be represented as a linear combination of the _____s.

The collection of quadratic polynomials with real coefficients has $\{1, t, t^2\}$ as a basis.

a. Meshfree methods

b. Basis function

c. Constructions of low-discrepancy sequences

d. Bernstein polynomial

20.   In mathematics, an _____ or member of a set is any one of the distinct objects that make up that set.

Writing A = {1,2,3,4}, means that the _____s of the set A are the numbers 1, 2, 3 and 4. Groups of _____s of A, for example {1,2}, are subsets of A.

   a. Universal code   b. Order
   c. Ideal   d. Element

21.   The mathematical concept of a _____ expresses the intuitive idea of deterministic dependence between two quantities, one of which is viewed as primary and the other as secondary. A _____ then is a way to associate a unique output for each input of a specified type, for example, a real number or an element of a given set.

   a. Function   b. Coherent
   c. Grill   d. Going up

22.   In mathematics, in the area of numerical analysis, _____ are a class of methods for converting a continuous operator problem (such as a differential equation) to a discrete problem. In principle, it is the equivalent of applying the method of variation to a function space, by converting the equation to a weak formulation. Typically one then applies some constraints on the functions space to characterize the space with a finite set of basis functions.

   a. Galerkin methods   b. Spectral methods
   c. Low-discrepancy sequence   d. Condition number

23.   In mathematics, a _____ is a rectangular table of elements, which may be numbers or, more generally, any abstract quantities that can be added and multiplied. Matrices are used to describe linear equations, keep track of the coefficients of linear transformations and to record data that depend on multiple parameters. Matrices are described by the field of _____ theory.

   a. Matrix   b. Double counting
   c. Compression   d. Coherent

24.   A pair x_k, y_k is called a data point and f is called an _____ for the data points.

When the numbers y_k are given by a known function f, we sometimes write f_k.

For example, suppose we have a table like this, which gives some values of an unknown function f.

   a. A Mathematical Theory of Communication   b. Interpolant
   c. A posteriori   d. A chemical equation

25.   Suppose that $\varphi : M \to N$ is a smooth map between smooth manifolds; then the _____ of φ at a point x is, in some sense, the best linear approximation of φ near x. It can be viewed as generalization of the total derivative of ordinary calculus. Explicitly, it is a linear map from the tangent space of M at x to the tangent space of N at φ

   a. Concurrent   b. Boundary
   c. Grill   d. Differential

26.   _____s arise in many problems in physics, engineering, etc. The following examples show how to solve _____s in a few simple cases when an exact solution exists.

A separable linear ordinary _____ of the first order has the general form:

$$\frac{dy}{dt} + f(t)y = 0$$

where f is some known function.

a. Nullcline

b. Homogeneous differential equation

c. Nahm equations

d. Differential equation

27. A _____ is a mathematical model of a system based on the use of a linear operator. _____s typically exhibit features and properties that are much simpler than the general, nonlinear case. As a mathematical abstraction or idealization, _____s find important applications in automatic control theory, signal processing, and telecommunications.

a. Percolation

b. Predispositioning Theory

c. Hybrid system

d. Linear system

28. In mathematics, the _____ is an approach to finding a particular solution to certain inhomogeneous ordinary differential equations and recurrence relations. It is closely related to the annihilator method, but instead of using a particular kind of differential operator in order to find the best possible form of the particular solution, a 'guess' is made as to the appropriate form, which is then tested by differentiating the resulting equation. In this sense, the _____ is less formal but more intuitive than the annihilator method.

a. Differential algebraic equations

b. Linear differential equation

c. Phase line

d. Method of undetermined coefficients

29. The _____ (_____, N_____, NU_____) (Schiesser, 1991; Hamdi, et al., 2007;) is a technique for solving partial differential equations (PDEs) where all but one dimension is discretized. The resulting semi-discrete problem is a set of ordinary differential equations (ODEs) or differential algebraic equations (DAEs) that is then integrated. A significant advantage of _____ is that it allows standard general purpose methods and software to be used that have been developed for the numerical integration of ODEs and DAEs.

a. Stiff equation

b. Method of lines

c. Semi-implicit Euler method

d. Roe approximate Riemann solver

30. _____ is a differential equation for which certain numerical methods for solving the equation are numerically unstable, unless the step size is taken to be extremely small.

a. 1-center problem

b. 120-cell

c. 2-3 heap

d. Stiff differential equation

31. In mathematics and computational science, the _____, named after Leonhard Euler, is a first order numerical procedure for solving ordinary differential equations with a given initial value. It is the most basic kind of explicit method for numerical integration for ordinary differential equations.

Consider the problem of calculating the shape of an unknown curve which starts at a given point and satisfies a given differential equation.

a. Uniform theory of diffraction   b. Analytic element method
c. Explicit and implicit methods   d. Euler method

32.   In mathematics, a _____ is a constant multiplicative factor of a certain object. For example, in the expression $9x^2$, the _____ of x^2 is 9.

The object can be such things as a variable, a vector, a function, etc.

a. Stability radius   b. Multivariate division algorithm
c. Fibonacci polynomials   d. Coefficient

33.   To define the derivative of a distribution, we first consider the case of a differentiable and integrable function $f : R \to R$. If φ is a _____, then we have

$$\int_{\mathbf{R}} f'\varphi \, dx = -\int_{\mathbf{R}} f\varphi' \, dx$$

using integration by parts (note that φ is zero outside of a bounded set and that therefore no boundary values have to be taken into account.) This suggests that if S is a distribution, we should define its derivative S' by

$$\langle S', \varphi \rangle = -\langle S, \varphi' \rangle.$$

a. Test function   b. Hyperfunction
c. Generalized functions   d. Schwartz kernel theorem

34.   In mathematics, a _____ on a vector space V is a bilinear mapping $V \times V \to F$, where F is the field of scalars. That is, a _____ is a function $B: V \times V \to F$ which is linear in each argument separately:

$$1. \ B(u + u', v) = B(u, v) + B(u', v),$$
$$2. \ B(u, v + v') = B(u, v) + B(u, v'),$$
$$3. \ B(\lambda u, v) = B(u, \lambda v) = \lambda B(u, v).$$

Any _____ on F^n can be expressed as

$$B(\mathbf{x}, \mathbf{y}) = \mathbf{x}^T A \mathbf{y} = \sum_{i,j=1}^{n} a_{ij} x_i y_j$$

where A is an n × n matrix.

The definition of a _____ can easily be extended to include modules over a commutative ring, with linear maps replaced by module homomorphisms.

a. 1-center problem   b. Degenerate form
c. 120-cell   d. Bilinear form

35.   In mathematics, an _____ is a statement about the relative size or order of two objects, or about whether they are the same or not

- The notation a < b means that a is less than b.
- The notation a > b means that a is greater than b.
- The notation a ≠ b means that a is not equal to b, but does not say that one is bigger than the other or even that they can be compared in size.

In all these cases, a is not equal to b, hence, '_____'.

These relations are known as strict _____

- The notation a ≤ b means that a is less than or equal to b;
- The notation a ≥ b means that a is greater than or equal to b;

An additional use of the notation is to show that one quantity is much greater than another, normally by several orders of magnitude.

- The notation a << b means that a is much less than b.
- The notation a >> b means that a is much greater than b.

If the sense of the _____ is the same for all values of the variables for which its members are defined, then the _____ is called an 'absolute' or 'unconditional' _____. If the sense of an _____ holds only for certain values of the variables involved, but is reversed or destroyed for other values of the variables, it is called a conditional _____.

An _____ may appear unsolvable because it only states whether a number is larger or smaller than another number; but it is possible to apply the same operations for equalities to inequalities. For example, to find x for the _____ 10x > 23 one would divide 23 by 10.

a. A posteriori   b. A Mathematical Theory of Communication
c. A chemical equation   d. Inequality

36.   In linear algebra, a _____ matrix is a matrix that is 'almost' a diagonal matrix. To be exact: a _____ matrix has nonzero elements only in the main diagonal, the first diagonal below this, and the first diagonal above the main diagonal.

For example, the following matrix is _____:

$$\begin{pmatrix} 1 & 4 & 0 & 0 \\ 3 & 4 & 1 & 0 \\ 0 & 2 & 3 & 4 \\ 0 & 0 & 1 & 3 \end{pmatrix}.$$

A determinant formed from a _____ matrix is known as a continuant.

a. Random matrix

b. Transition matrix

c. Pascal matrix

d. Tridiagonal

1. In mathematics, a _____ is a vector space of functions equipped with a norm that is a combination of L^p norms of the function itself as well as its derivatives up to a given order. The derivatives are understood in a suitable weak sense to make the space complete, thus a Banach space. Intuitively, a _____ is a Banach space or Hilbert space of functions with sufficiently many derivatives for some application domain, such as partial differential equations, and equipped with a norm that measures both the size and smoothness of a function.

   a. Sobolev space   b. 2-3 heap
   c. 120-cell   d. 1-center problem

2. In mathematics, especially in the area of abstract algebra known as ring theory, a _____ is a ring with $0 \neq 1$ such that $ab = 0$ implies that either $a = 0$ or $b = 0$. That is, it is a nontrivial ring without left or right zero divisors. A commutative _____ is called an integral _____.

   a. Modular representation theory   b. Simple ring
   c. Left primitive ring   d. Domain

3. Initial objects are also called _____, and terminal objects are also called final.

   a. Colimit   b. Coterminal
   c. Terminal object   d. Direct limit

4. In mathematics, in the field of differential equations, an _____ is an ordinary differential equation together with specified value, called the initial condition, of the unknown function at a given point in the domain of the solution. In physics or other sciences, modeling a system frequently amounts to solving an _____; in this context, the differential equation is an evolution equation specifying how, given initial conditions, the system will evolve with time.

An _____ is a differential equation

$$y'(t) = f(t, y(t)) \quad \text{with} \quad f : \mathbb{R} \times \mathbb{R} \to \mathbb{R}$$

together with a point in the domain of f

$$(t_0, y_0) \in \mathbb{R} \times \mathbb{R},$$

called the initial condition.

   a. Initial value problem   b. A chemical equation
   c. A posteriori   d. A Mathematical Theory of Communication

5. In physics, an _____ is a function acting on the space of physical states. As a result of its application on a physical state, another physical state is obtained, very often along with some extra relevant information.

The simplest example of the utility of _____s is the study of symmetry.

   a. Affine Hecke algebra   b. Operator
   c. Operand   d. Algebraic signal processing

6. _____ is an important second-order linear partial differential equation that describes the propagation of a variety of waves, such as sound waves, light waves and water waves. It arises in fields such as acoustics, electromagnetics, and fluid dynamics. Historically, the problem of a vibrating string such as that of a musical instrument was studied by Jean le Rond d'Alembert, Leonhard Euler, Daniel Bernoulli, and Joseph-Louis Lagrange.

a. The wave equation
b. Dispersion relations
c. Cauchy momentum equation
d. Geodesic

7. The _____ , is achieved in a packed stadium when successive groups of spectators briefly stand and raise their arms. Each spectator is required to rise at the same time as those straight in front and behind, and slightly after the person immediately to either the right or the left. Immediately upon stretching to full height, the spectator returns to the usual seated position.

a. Wave
b. Lagrangian
c. Thermodynamic limit
d. Pauli exclusion principle

8. The _____ is an important second-order linear partial differential equation that describes the propagation of a variety of waves, such as sound waves, light waves and water waves. It arises in fields such as acoustics, electromagnetics, and fluid dynamics. Historically, the problem of a vibrating string such as that of a musical instrument was studied by Jean le Rond d'Alembert, Leonhard Euler, Daniel Bernoulli, and Joseph-Louis Lagrange.

a. Lagrangian
b. Wave equation
c. Random walk
d. Cauchy momentum equation

9. In linear algebra, _____ is an efficient algorithm for solving systems of linear equations, finding the rank of a matrix, and calculating the inverse of an invertible square matrix. _____ is named after German mathematician and scientist Carl Friedrich Gauss.

Elementary row operations are used to reduce a matrix to row echelon form.

a. Crout matrix decomposition
b. Conjugate gradient method
c. Cholesky decomposition
d. Gaussian elimination

10. The requirement that L have strictly positive diagonal entries can be dropped to extend the factorization to the positive semidefinite case. The statement then reads: a square matrix A has a Cholesky decomposition if and only if A is Hermitian and positive semi-definite. _____ for positive semidefinite matrices are not unique in general.

a. Singular values
b. Positive definite kernel
c. Wold decomposition
d. Cholesky factorizations

11. In mathematical analysis, the _____ is the collection of functions

$$D_n(x) = \sum_{k=-n}^{n} e^{ikx} = 1 + 2\sum_{k=1}^{n} \cos(kx) = \frac{\sin\left(\left(n+\frac{1}{2}\right)x\right)}{\sin(x/2)}.$$

It is named after Johann Peter Gustav Lejeune Dirichlet.

The importance of the _____ comes from its relation to Fourier series. The convolution of $D_n\pi$ is the nth-degree Fourier series approximation to f.

a. Dirichlet kernel

b. Constructive analysis

c. Total variation

d. Mountain pass theorem

12.   In the various branches of mathematics that fall under the heading of abstract algebra, the _____ of a homomorphism measures the degree to which the homomorphism fails to be injective. An important special case is the _____ of a matrix, also called the null space.

The definition of _____ takes various forms in various contexts.

a. Kernel

b. Bertrand paradox

c. Constructivism

d. Leibniz formula

13.   In mathematics, a _____ decomposes a periodic function into a sum of simple oscillating functions, namely sines and cosines. The study of _____ is a branch of Fourier analysis. _____ were introduced by Joseph Fourier for the purpose of solving the heat equation in a metal plate.

a. Fourier series

b. 1-center problem

c. Triangle wave

d. Fourier series of a periodic function converges

14.   In mathematics, a _____ is often represented as the sum of a sequence of terms. That is, a _____ is represented as a list of numbers with addition operations between them, for example this arithmetic sequence:

$$1 + 2 + 3 + 4 + 5 + ... + 99 + 100$$

In most cases of interest the terms of the sequence are produced according to a certain rule, such as by a formula, by an algorithm, by a sequence of measurements, or even by a random number generator.

a. Concavity

b. Contact

c. Blind

d. Series

15.   A vibration in a string is a wave. Usually a _____ produces a sound whose frequency in most cases is constant. Therefore, since frequency characterizes the pitch, the sound produced is a constant note.

a. 120-cell

b. Vibrating string

c. Harmonic oscillator

d. 1-center problem

16.   In statistics the _____ of an event i is the number n_i of times the event occurred in the experiment or the study. These frequencies are often graphically represented in histograms.

We speak of absolute frequencies, when the counts n_i themselves are given and of

$$f_i = \frac{n_i}{N} = \frac{n_i}{\sum_i n_i}$$

Taking the f_i for all i and tabulating or plotting them leads to a _____ distribution.

   a. Subharmonic   b. Robinson-Dadson curves
   c. Digital room correction   d. Frequency

17.   In statistics, the _____ is the value that occurs the most frequently in a data set or a probability distribution. In some fields, notably education, sample data are often called scores, and the sample _____ is known as the modal score.

Like the statistical mean and the median, the _____ is a way of capturing important information about a random variable or a population in a single quantity.

   a. Mode   b. Function
   c. Deltoid   d. Field

18.   In mathematics, specifically in combinatorial commutative algebra, a convex lattice polytope P is called _____ if it has the following property: given any positive integer n, every lattice point of the dilation nP, obtained from P by scaling its vertices by the factor n and taking the convex hull of the resulting points, can be written as the sum of exactly n lattice points in P. This property plays an important role in the theory of toric varieties, where it corresponds to projective normality of the toric variety determined by P.

The simplex in R^k with the vertices at the origin and along the unit coordinate vectors is _____.

   a. Normal   b. Demihypercubes
   c. Polytetrahedron   d. Hypercube

19.   A _____ of an oscillating system is a pattern of motion in which all parts of the system move sinusoidally with the same frequency. The frequencies of the _____s of a system are known as its natural frequencies or resonant frequencies. A physical object, such as a building or a bridge or a molecule, has a set of _____s that depend on its structure and composition.

   a. Separation of variables   b. Total differential equation
   c. Normal mode   d. Boundary value problem

20.   In mathematics, the _____, name after Ivar Fredholm, is one of Fredholm's theorems and is a result in Fredholm theory. It may be expressed in several ways, as a theorem of linear algebra, a theorem of integral equations, or as a theorem on Fredholm operators. Part of the result states that, a non-zero complex number in the spectrum of a compact operator is an eigenvalue.

   a. Liouville-Neumann series   b. Fredholm alternative
   c. Fredholm operator   d. Fredholm integral equation

21.   A _____ is a wave that remains in a constant position. This phenomenon can occur because the medium is moving in the opposite direction to the wave, or it can arise in a stationary medium as a result of interference between two waves traveling in opposite directions. In the second case, for waves of equal amplitude travelling in opposing directions, there is on average no net propagation of energy.

a. Transverse mode
c. Standing wave

b. Wave impedance
d. Wavenumber-frequency diagram

22.   In mathematics, the _____ or Pythagoras' theorem is a relation in Euclidean geometry among the three sides of a right triangle. The theorem is named after the Greek mathematician Pythagoras, who by tradition is credited with its discovery and proof, although it is often argued that knowledge of the theory predates him.. The theorem is as follows:

In any right triangle, the area of the square whose side is the hypotenuse is equal to the sum of the areas of the squares whose sides are the two legs.

a. 2-3 heap
c. 1-center problem

b. Pythagorean theorem
d. 120-cell

23.   In physics, _____ is the tendency of a system to oscillate at maximum amplitude at certain frequencies, known as the system's _____ frequencies. At these frequencies, even small periodic driving forces can produce large amplitude vibrations, because the system stores vibrational energy. When damping is small, the _____ frequency is approximately equal to the natural frequency of the system, which is the frequency of free vibrations.

a. Sawtooth wave
c. Signal compression

b. Square wave
d. Resonance

24.   In mathematics, a _____ is a statement that can be proved on the basis of explicitly stated or previously agreed assumptions.

a. Boolean function
c. Theorem

b. Logical value
d. Disjunction introduction

25.   The mathematical concept of a _____ expresses the intuitive idea of deterministic dependence between two quantities, one of which is viewed as primary and the other as secondary. A _____ then is a way to associate a unique output for each input of a specified type, for example, a real number or an element of a given set.

a. Going up
c. Function

b. Coherent
d. Grill

26.   To define the derivative of a distribution, we first consider the case of a differentiable and integrable function $f : R \rightarrow R$. If φ is a _____, then we have

$$\int_{\mathbf{R}} f' \varphi \, dx = - \int_{\mathbf{R}} f \varphi' \, dx$$

using integration by parts (note that φ is zero outside of a bounded set and that therefore no boundary values have to be taken into account.) This suggests that if S is a distribution, we should define its derivative S' by

$$\langle S', \varphi \rangle = - \langle S, \varphi' \rangle.$$

a. Schwartz kernel theorem
c. Hyperfunction

b. Generalized functions
d. Test function

27. In mathematics, in the area of numerical analysis, _____ are a class of methods for converting a continuous operator problem (such as a differential equation) to a discrete problem. In principle, it is the equivalent of applying the method of variation to a function space, by converting the equation to a weak formulation. Typically one then applies some constraints on the functions space to characterize the space with a finite set of basis functions.
   a. Low-discrepancy sequence   b. Spectral methods
   c. Galerkin methods   d. Condition number

28. _____ is a core concept of basic mathematics, specifically in the fields of infinitesimal calculus and mathematical analysis. Given a function f

$$\int_a^b f(x)\,dx\,,$$

is equal to the area of a region in the xy-plane bounded by the graph of f, the x-axis, and the vertical lines x = a and x = b, with areas below the x-axis being subtracted.

The term 'integral' may also refer to the notion of antiderivative, a function F whose derivative is the given function f.

   a. OMAC   b. Integration
   c. Epigraph   d. Apex

29. In calculus, and more generally in mathematical analysis, _____ is a rule that transforms the integral of products of functions into other, hopefully simpler, integrals. The rule arises from the product rule of differentiation.

If u = f[x], v = g[x], and the differentials du = f '[x] dx and dv = g'[x] dx; then in its simplest form the product rule is:

[×]>

   a. Integral test for convergence   b. Integration by parts operator
   c. Integration by parts   d. Arc length

30. In mathematics, a _____ is a rectangular table of elements, which may be numbers or, more generally, any abstract quantities that can be added and multiplied. Matrices are used to describe linear equations, keep track of the coefficients of linear transformations and to record data that depend on multiple parameters. Matrices are described by the field of _____ theory.
   a. Matrix   b. Compression
   c. Double counting   d. Coherent

31. In commutative algebra, the notions of an element _____ over a ring, and of an _____ extension of rings, are a generalization of the notions in field theory of an element being algebraic over a field, and of an algebraic extension of fields.

The special case of greatest interest in number theory is that of complex numbers _____ over the ring of integers Z.

The term ring will be understood to mean commutative ring with a unit.

a. Integral
c. Antidifferentiation

b. Integral test for convergence
d. Arc length

32.   A pair x_k, y_k is called a data point and f is called an _____ for the data points.

When the numbers y_k are given by a known function f, we sometimes write f_k.

For example, suppose we have a table like this, which gives some values of an unknown function f.

a. A chemical equation
c. A posteriori

b. A Mathematical Theory of Communication
d. Interpolant

33.   In mathematics and computational science, the _____, named after Leonhard Euler, is a first order numerical procedure for solving ordinary differential equations with a given initial value. It is the most basic kind of explicit method for numerical integration for ordinary differential equations.

Consider the problem of calculating the shape of an unknown curve which starts at a given point and satisfies a given differential equation.

a. Analytic element method
c. Explicit and implicit methods

b. Uniform theory of diffraction
d. Euler method

34.   The _____ or Dirac's delta is a mathematical construct introduced by the British theoretical physicist Paul Dirac. Informally, it is a function representing an infinitely sharp peak bounding unit area: a function that has the value zero everywhere except at x = 0 where its value is infinitely large in such a way that its total integral is 1. It is a continuous analogue of the discrete Kronecker delta.
a. Weak derivative
c. Hyperfunction

b. Schwartz kernel theorem
d. Dirac delta

35.   A _____ is a single identifiable localized source of something. A _____ has negligible extent, distinguishing it from other source geometries. Sources are called _____s because in mathematical modeling, these sources can usually be approximated as a mathematical point to simplify analysis.
a. 1-center problem
c. Point source

b. 2-3 heap
d. 120-cell

1. In mathematics, the _____, name after Ivar Fredholm, is one of Fredholm's theorems and is a result in Fredholm theory. It may be expressed in several ways, as a theorem of linear algebra, a theorem of integral equations, or as a theorem on Fredholm operators. Part of the result states that, a non-zero complex number in the spectrum of a compact operator is an eigenvalue.
   a. Fredholm integral equation
   b. Liouville-Neumann series
   c. Fredholm alternative
   d. Fredholm operator

2. _____ is a branch of mathematics that includes the study of limits, derivatives, integrals, and infinite series, and constitutes a major part of modern university education. Historically, it has been referred to as 'the _____ of infinitesimals', or 'infinitesimal _____'. Most basically, _____ is the study of change, in the same way that geometry is the study of space.
   a. Calculus
   b. Hyperbolic angle
   c. Partial sum
   d. Test for Divergence

3. The _____ specifies the relationship between the two central operations of calculus, differentiation and integration.

   The first part of the theorem, sometimes called the first _____, shows that an indefinite integration can be reversed by a differentiation.

   The second part, sometimes called the second _____, allows one to compute the definite integral of a function by using any one of its infinitely many antiderivatives.

   a. Hyperbolic angle
   b. Maxima and minima
   c. Fundamental theorem of calculus
   d. Standard part function

4. In mathematics, a _____ is a statement that can be proved on the basis of explicitly stated or previously agreed assumptions.
   a. Logical value
   b. Theorem
   c. Boolean function
   d. Disjunction introduction

5. In mathematics, a _____ is a vector space of functions equipped with a norm that is a combination of L^p norms of the function itself as well as its derivatives up to a given order. The derivatives are understood in a suitable weak sense to make the space complete, thus a Banach space. Intuitively, a _____ is a Banach space or Hilbert space of functions with sufficiently many derivatives for some application domain, such as partial differential equations, and equipped with a norm that measures both the size and smoothness of a function.
   a. 1-center problem
   b. 120-cell
   c. 2-3 heap
   d. Sobolev space

6. In commutative algebra, the notions of an element _____ over a ring, and of an _____ extension of rings, are a generalization of the notions in field theory of an element being algebraic over a field, and of an algebraic extension of fields.

   The special case of greatest interest in number theory is that of complex numbers _____ over the ring of integers Z.

   The term ring will be understood to mean commutative ring with a unit.

a. Antidifferentiation
c. Arc length

b. Integral test for convergence
d. Integral

7.   In mathematics, specifically in combinatorial commutative algebra, a convex lattice polytope P is called _____ if it has the following property: given any positive integer n, every lattice point of the dilation nP, obtained from P by scaling its vertices by the factor n and taking the convex hull of the resulting points, can be written as the sum of exactly n lattice points in P. This property plays an important role in the theory of toric varieties, where it corresponds to projective normality of the toric variety determined by P.

The simplex in R^k with the vertices at the origin and along the unit coordinate vectors is _____.

a. Hypercube
c. Polytetrahedron

b. Demihypercubes
d. Normal

8.   A surface normal to a flat surface is a vector which is perpendicular to that surface. A normal to a non-flat surface at a point P on the surface is a vector perpendicular to the tangent plane to that surface at P. The word 'normal' is also used as an adjective: a line normal to a plane, the normal component of a force, the _____, etc.

a. Normal vector
c. Torus

b. Real projective plane
d. Prolate spheroid

9.   In physics and in _____ calculus, a _____ is a concept characterized by a magnitude and a direction. A _____ can be thought of as an arrow in Euclidean space, drawn from an initial point A pointing to a terminal point B.

a. Constraint
c. Deviation

b. Dominance
d. Vector

10.   The _____ of any solid, plasma, vacuum or theoretical object is how much three-dimensional space it occupies, often quantified numerically. One-dimensional figures and two-dimensional shapes are assigned zero _____ in the three-dimensional space. _____ is presented as ml or cm^3.

_____s of straight-edged and circular shapes are calculated using arithmetic formulae.

a. Cauchy momentum equation
c. Volume

b. Thermodynamic limit
d. Stress-energy tensor

11.   In mathematical analysis, the _____ is the collection of functions

$$D_n(x) = \sum_{k=-n}^{n} e^{ikx} = 1 + 2\sum_{k=1}^{n} \cos(kx) = \frac{\sin\left(\left(n + \frac{1}{2}\right)x\right)}{\sin(x/2)}.$$

It is named after Johann Peter Gustav Lejeune Dirichlet.

The importance of the _____ comes from its relation to Fourier series. The convolution of $D_n\pi$ is the nth-degree Fourier series approximation to f.

a. Dirichlet kernel   b. Total variation
c. Mountain pass theorem   d. Constructive analysis

12. _____ is a quantity expressing the two-dimensional size of a defined part of a surface, typically a region bounded by a closed curve. The term surface _____ refers to the total _____ of the exposed surface of a 3-dimensional solid, such as the sum of the _____s of the exposed sides of a polyhedron. _____ is an important invariant in the differential geometry of surfaces.

a. A chemical equation   b. A Mathematical Theory of Communication
c. A posteriori   d. Area

13. In vector calculus, the _____ is an operator that measures the magnitude of a vector field's source or sink at a given point; the _____ of a vector field is a scalar. For example, for a vector field that denotes the velocity of air expanding as it is heated, the _____ of the velocity field would have a positive value because the air expands. If the air cools and contracts, the _____ is negative.

a. Helmholtz decomposition   b. Del operator
c. Vector field reconstruction   d. Divergence

14. In abstract algebra, a _____ is an algebraic structure in which the operations of addition, subtraction, multiplication and division may be performed in a way that satisfies some familiar rules from the arithmetic of ordinary numbers.

All _____s are rings, but not conversely. _____s differ from rings most importantly in the requirement that division be possible, but also, in modern definitions, by the requirement that the multiplication operation in a _____ be commutative.

a. Chord   b. Functional
c. Blind   d. Field

15. In the various branches of mathematics that fall under the heading of abstract algebra, the _____ of a homomorphism measures the degree to which the homomorphism fails to be injective. An important special case is the _____ of a matrix, also called the null space.

The definition of _____ takes various forms in various contexts.

a. Bertrand paradox   b. Leibniz formula
c. Constructivism   d. Kernel

16. In mathematics, a _____ is an integral where the function to be integrated is evaluated along a curve. Various different _____s are in use. In the case of a closed curve in two dimensions or the complex plane it is also called a contour integral.

a. Line integral   b. Cauchy integral theorem
c. Bispectrum   d. Hankel contour

17. In physics, an _____ is a function acting on the space of physical states. As a result of its application on a physical state, another physical state is obtained, very often along with some extra relevant information.

The simplest example of the utility of _____s is the study of symmetry.

a. Algebraic signal processing   b. Operator

c. Affine Hecke algebra   d. Operand

18. In mathematics, specifically in topology, a _____ is a two-dimensional manifold. The most familiar examples are those that arise as the boundaries of solid objects in ordinary three-dimensional Euclidean space, EÂ³. On the other hand, there are also more exotic _____s, that are so 'contorted' that they cannot be embedded in three-dimensional space at all.

a. Homoeoid   b. Standard torus

c. Cross-cap   d. Surface

19. In mathematics, a _____ is a definite integral taken over a surface; it can be thought of as the double integral analog of the line integral. Given a surface, one may integrate over it scalar fields, and vector fields.

_____s have applications in physics, particularly with the classical theory of electromagnetism.

a. Shift theorem   b. Surface integral

c. Laplacian   d. Differentiation operator

20. In mathematics a _____ is a construction in vector calculus which associates a vector to every point in a Euclidean space.

_____s are often used in physics to model, for example, the speed and direction of a moving fluid throughout space, or the strength and direction of some force, such as the magnetic or gravitational force, as it changes from point to point.

In the rigorous mathematical treatment, _____s are defined on manifolds as sections of a manifold's tangent bundle.

a. 120-cell   b. 1-center problem

c. Vector field   d. 2-3 heap

21. The _____ of a material is defined as its mass per unit volume:

$$\rho = \frac{m}{V}$$

Different materials usually have different densities, so _____ is an important concept regarding buoyancy, metal purity and packaging.

In some cases _____ is expressed as the dimensionless quantities specific gravity or relative _____, in which case it is expressed in multiples of the _____ of some other standard material, usually water or air.

In a well-known story, Archimedes was given the task of determining whether King Hiero's goldsmith was embezzling gold during the manufacture of a wreath dedicated to the gods and replacing it with another, cheaper alloy.

a. 2-3 heap   b. 1-center problem
c. 120-cell   d. Density

22.   In the various subfields of physics, there exist two common usages of the term _____, both with rigorous mathematical frameworks.

- In the study of transport phenomena, _____ is defined as the amount that flows through a unit area per unit time. _____ in this definition is a vector.
- In the field of electromagnetism, _____ is usually the integral of a vector quantity over a finite surface. The result of this integration is a scalar quantity. The magnetic _____ is thus the integral of the magnetic vector field B over a surface, and the electric _____ is defined similarly. Using this definition, the _____ of the Poynting vector over a specified surface is the rate at which electromagnetic energy flows through that surface. Confusingly, the Poynting vector is sometimes called the power _____, which is an example of the first usage of _____, above. It has units of watts per square metre

One could argue, based on the work of James Clerk Maxwell, that the transport definition precedes the more recent way the term is used in electromagnetism. The specific quote from Maxwell is 'In the case of _____es, we have to take the integral, over a surface, of the _____ through every element of the surface. The result of this operation is called the surface integral of the _____.

a. 1-center problem   b. Flux
c. 120-cell   d. Rotational speed

23.   In physics, _____, k, is the property of a material that indicates its ability to conduct heat. It appears primarily in Fourier's Law for heat conduction.

First, we define heat conduction by the formula:

$$H = \frac{\Delta Q}{\Delta t} = k \times A \times \frac{\Delta T}{x}$$

where $\dfrac{\Delta Q}{\Delta t}$ is the rate of heat flow, k is the _____, A is the total cross sectional area of conducting surface, ΔT is temperature difference and x is the thickness of conducting surface separating the 2 temperatures.

a. 2-3 heap   b. 120-cell
c. 1-center problem   d. Thermal conductivity

24.   In differential geometry there are a number of second-order, linear, elliptic differential operators bearing the name
_____

The connection _____ is a differential operator acting on the various tensor bundles of a manifold, defined in terms of a Riemmanian- or pseudo-Riemannian metric.

a. Differential operator
b. Multivariable calculus
c. Shift theorem
d. Laplacian

25. _____ is a fundamental construction of differential calculus and admits many possible generalizations within the fields of mathematical analysis, combinatorics, algebra, and geometry.

In real, complex, and functional analysis, _____s are generalized to functions of several real or complex variables and functions between topological vector spaces. An important case is the variational _____ in the calculus of variations.

a. Derivative
b. Functional derivative
c. Lin-Tsien equation
d. Metric derivative

26. A _____ is a directional derivative taken in the direction normal (that is, orthogonal) to some surface in space, or more generally along a normal vector field orthogonal to some hypersurface. See for example Neumann boundary condition. If the normal direction is denoted by $\vec{n}$, then the directional derivative of a function f is sometimes denoted as $\dfrac{\partial f}{\partial n}$.

a. Differentiation under the integral sign
b. Gradient
c. Point of inflection
d. Normal derivative

27. The _____ is an important partial differential equation which describes the distribution of heat in a given region over time. For a function u

$$\frac{\partial u}{\partial t} - k \left(\frac{\partial^2 u}{\partial x^2} + \frac{\partial^2 u}{\partial y^2} + \frac{\partial^2 u}{\partial z^2} \right) = 0$$

where k is a constant.

The _____ is of fundamental importance in diverse scientific fields.

a. 2-3 heap
b. 1-center problem
c. 120-cell
d. Heat equation

28. _____ is a core concept of basic mathematics, specifically in the fields of infinitesimal calculus and mathematical analysis. Given a function f

$$\int_a^b f(x)\, dx \,,$$

is equal to the area of a region in the xy-plane bounded by the graph of f, the x-axis, and the vertical lines x = a and x = b, with areas below the x-axis being subtracted.

The term 'integral' may also refer to the notion of antiderivative, a function F whose derivative is the given function f.

   a. OMAC   b. Epigraph

   c. Apex   d. Integration

29.   In calculus, and more generally in mathematical analysis, _____ is a rule that transforms the integral of products of functions into other, hopefully simpler, integrals. The rule arises from the product rule of differentiation.

If u = f[x], v = g[x], and the differentials du = f '[x] dx and dv = g'[x] dx; then in its simplest form the product rule is:

   a. Integration by parts   b. Arc length

   c. Integration by parts operator   d. Integral test for convergence

30.   In mathematics, the term _____ has several different important meanings:

- An _____ is an equality that remains true regardless of the values of any variables that appear within it, to distinguish it from an equality which is true under more particular conditions. For this, the 'triple bar' symbol ≡ is sometimes used.
- In algebra, an _____ or _____ element of a set S with a binary operation Â· is an element e that, when combined with any element x of S, produces that same x. That is, eÂ·x = xÂ·e = x for all x in S.
  - The _____ function from a set S to itself, often denoted id or id$_S$, s the function such that i = x for all x in S. This function serves as the _____ element in the set of all functions from S to itself with respect to function composition.
  - In linear algebra, the _____ matrix of size n is the n-by-n square matrix with ones on the main diagonal and zeros elsewhere. This matrix serves as the _____ with respect to matrix multiplication.

A common example of the first meaning is the trigonometric _____

$$\sin^2 \theta + \cos^2 \theta = 1$$

which is true for all real values of θ, as opposed to

$$\cos \theta = 1,$$

which is true only for some values of θ, not all. For example, the latter equation is true when $\theta = 0$, false when $\theta = 2$

The concepts of 'additive _____' and 'multiplicative _____' are central to the Peano axioms. The number 0 is the 'additive _____' for integers, real numbers, and complex numbers. For the real numbers, for all $a \in \mathbb{R}$,

$$0 + a = a,$$

$$a + 0 = a, \text{ and}$$

$$0 + 0 = 0.$$

Similarly, The number 1 is the 'multiplicative _____' for integers, real numbers, and complex numbers.

a. Intersection

b. Identity

c. ARIA

d. Action

31.   The _____ governs the differentiation of products of differentiable functions.

a. 120-cell

b. Reciprocal Rule

c. Product rule

d. 1-center problem

32.   In mathematics, a _____ decomposes a periodic function into a sum of simple oscillating functions, namely sines and cosines. The study of _____ is a branch of Fourier analysis. _____ were introduced by Joseph Fourier for the purpose of solving the heat equation in a metal plate.

a. Triangle wave

b. 1-center problem

c. Fourier series

d. Fourier series of a periodic function converges

33.   In mathematics, especially in the area of abstract algebra known as ring theory, a _____ is a ring with 0 ≠ 1 such that ab = 0 implies that either a = 0 or b = 0. That is, it is a nontrivial ring without left or right zero divisors. A commutative _____ is called an integral _____.

a. Simple ring

b. Left primitive ring

c. Modular representation theory

d. Domain

34.   In mathematics, a _____ is often represented as the sum of a sequence of terms. That is, a _____ is represented as a list of numbers with addition operations between them, for example this arithmetic sequence:

1 + 2 + 3 + 4 + 5 + ... + 99 + 100

In most cases of interest the terms of the sequence are produced according to a certain rule, such as by a formula, by an algorithm, by a sequence of measurements, or even by a random number generator.

a. Contact

b. Series

c. Blind

d. Concavity

35.   In mathematics, _____ is any of several methods for solving ordinary and partial differential equations, in which algebra allows one to re-write an equation so that each of two variables occurs on a different side of the equation.

Suppose a differential equation can be written in the form

$$\frac{d}{dx}f(x) = g(x)h(f(x)), \qquad (1)$$

which we can write more simply by letting y = f:

$$\frac{dy}{dx} = g(x)h(y).$$

As long as h≠ 0, we can rearrange terms to obtain:

$$\frac{dy}{h(y)} = g(x)dx,$$

so that the two variables x and y have been separated.

Some who dislike Leibniz's notation may prefer to write this as

$$\frac{1}{h(y)}\frac{dy}{dx} = g(x),$$

but that fails to make it quite as obvious why this is called '_____'.

   a. Normal mode   b. Wronskian
   c. Separation of variables   d. Sturm-Liouville equation

36. In mathematics, an _____ is a statement about the relative size or order of two objects, or about whether they are the same or not

- The notation a < b means that a is less than b.
- The notation a > b means that a is greater than b.
- The notation a ≠ b means that a is not equal to b, but does not say that one is bigger than the other or even that they can be compared in size.

In all these cases, a is not equal to b, hence, '_____'.

These relations are known as strict _____

- The notation a ≤ b means that a is less than or equal to b;
- The notation a ≥ b means that a is greater than or equal to b;

An additional use of the notation is to show that one quantity is much greater than another, normally by several orders of magnitude.

- The notation a << b means that a is much less than b.
- The notation a >> b means that a is much greater than b.

If the sense of the _____ is the same for all values of the variables for which its members are defined, then the _____ is called an 'absolute' or 'unconditional' _____. If the sense of an _____ holds only for certain values of the variables involved, but is reversed or destroyed for other values of the variables, it is called a conditional _____.

An _____ may appear unsolvable because it only states whether a number is larger or smaller than another number; but it is possible to apply the same operations for equalities to inequalities. For example, to find x for the _____ 10x > 23 one would divide 23 by 10.

a. A posteriori
b. A Mathematical Theory of Communication
c. Inequality
d. A chemical equation

37. The _____ of an angle is the ratio of the length of the opposite side to the length of the hypotenuse. In our case

$$\sin A = \frac{\text{opposite}}{\text{hypotenuse}} = \frac{a}{h} \, .$$

Note that this ratio does not depend on size of the particular right triangle chosen, as long as it contains the angle A, since all such triangles are similar.

The cosine of an angle is the ratio of the length of the adjacent side to the length of the hypotenuse.

a. Trigonometric functions
b. Right angle
c. Law of sines
d. Sine

38. The requirement that L have strictly positive diagonal entries can be dropped to extend the factorization to the positive semidefinite case. The statement then reads: a square matrix A has a Cholesky decomposition if and only if A is Hermitian and positive semi-definite. _____ for positive semidefinite matrices are not unique in general.
a. Wold decomposition
b. Singular values
c. Positive definite kernel
d. Cholesky factorizations

39. In geometry, a _____ is the region in a plane bounded by a circle.

A _____ is said to be closed or open according to whether or not it contains the circle that constitutes its boundary. In Cartesian coordinates, the open _____ of center and radius R is given by the formula

$$D = \{(x, y) \in \mathbb{R}^2 : (x - a)^2 + (y - b)^2 < R^2\}$$

while the closed _____ of the same center and radius is given by

$$\overline{D} = \{(x, y) \in \mathbb{R}^2 : (x - a)^2 + (y - b)^2 \leq R^2\}.$$

The area of a closed or open _____ of radius R is πR².

   a. Boussinesq approximation   b. Congruent
   c. Disk   d. Deltoid

   40.   In calculus, the _____ is a formula for the derivative of the composite of two functions.

In intuitive terms, if a variable, y, depends on a second variable, u, which in turn depends on a third variable, x, then the rate of change of y with respect to x can be computed as the rate of change of y with respect to u multiplied by the rate of change of u with respect to x. Schematically,

$$\frac{dy}{dx} = \frac{dy}{du} \cdot \frac{du}{dx}.$$

For an explanation of notation used in this section, see Function composition.

The _____ states that, under appropriate conditions,

$$(f \circ g)'(x) = f'(g(x))g'(x),$$

which in short form is written as

$$(f \circ g)' = f' \circ g \cdot g'.$$

Alternatively, in the Leibniz notation, the _____ is

$$\frac{dy}{dx} = \frac{dy}{du} \cdot \frac{du}{dx}.$$

In integration, the counterpart to the _____ is the substitution rule.

a. Chain rule

b. 120-cell

c. 1-center problem

d. Product rule

41.   In mathematics, the _____ system is a two-dimensional coordinate system in which each point on a plane is determined by an angle and a distance. The _____ system is especially useful in situations where the relationship between two points is most easily expressed in terms of angles and distance; in the more familiar Cartesian or rectangular coordinate system, such a relationship can only be found through trigonometric formulation.

As the coordinate system is two-dimensional, each point is determined by two _____s: the radial coordinate and the angular coordinate.

a. Sequence alignment

b. Sir Isaac Newton

c. Vampire

d. Polar coordinate

42.   In mathematics, an _____ in the sense of ring theory is a subring $\mathcal{O}$ of a ring R that satisfies the conditions

1.   R is a ring which is a finite-dimensional algebra over the rational number field $\mathbb{Q}$
2. $\mathcal{O}$ spans R over $\mathbb{Q}$, so that $\mathbb{Q}\mathcal{O} = R$, and
3. $\mathcal{O}$ is a lattice in R.

The third condition can be stated more accurately, in terms of the extension of scalars of R to the real numbers, embedding R in a real vector space. In less formal terms, additively $\mathcal{O}$ should be a free abelian group generated by a basis for R over $\mathbb{Q}$.

The leading example is the case where R is a number field K and $\mathcal{O}$ is its ring of integers. In algebraic number theory there are examples for any K other than the rational field of proper subrings of the ring of integers that are also _____s.

a. Algebraic

b. Annihilator

c. Efficiency

d. Order

43.   In mathematics, a _____ is an infinite series of the form

$$f(x) = \sum_{n=0}^{\infty} a_n (x - c)^n = a_0 + a_1 (x - c)^1 + a_2 (x - c)^2 + a_3 (x - c)^3 + \cdots$$

where a_n represents the coefficient of the nth term, c is a constant, and x varies around c

In many situations c is equal to zero, for instance when considering a Maclaurin series.

a. Polylogarithmic

b. Power series

c. Smooth infinitesimal analysis

d. Cauchy principal value

44. In mathematics, _____, first defined by the mathematician Daniel Bernoulli and generalized by Friedrich Bessel, are canonical solutions ys differential equation:

$$x^2 \frac{d^2 y}{dx^2} + x \frac{dy}{dx} + (x^2 - \alpha^2) y = 0$$

for an arbitrary real or complex number α. The most common and important special case is where α is an integer n.

Although α and −α produce the same differential equation, it is conventional to define different _____ for these two orders.

a. Jack function

b. Legendre chi function

c. Mittag-Leffler function

d. Bessel functions

45. The mathematical concept of a _____ expresses the intuitive idea of deterministic dependence between two quantities, one of which is viewed as primary and the other as secondary. A _____ then is a way to associate a unique output for each input of a specified type, for example, a real number or an element of a given set.

a. Coherent

b. Function

c. Going up

d. Grill

46. In mathematics, the _____s are analogs of the ordinary trigonometric functions. The basic _____s are the hyperbolic sine 'sinh', and the hyperbolic cosine 'cosh', from which are derived the hyperbolic tangent 'tanh', etc., in analogy to the derived trigonometric functions. The inverse _____ are the area hyperbolic sine 'arsinh' (also called 'asinh', or sometimes by the misnomer of 'arcsinh') and so on.

a. Hyperbolic function

b. Heaviside step function

c. Square root

d. Rectangular function

47. In mathematics, in the area of numerical analysis, _____ are a class of methods for converting a continuous operator problem (such as a differential equation) to a discrete problem. In principle, it is the equivalent of applying the method of variation to a function space, by converting the equation to a weak formulation. Typically one then applies some constraints on the functions space to characterize the space with a finite set of basis functions.

a. Low-discrepancy sequence

b. Spectral methods

c. Condition number

d. Galerkin methods

48. In signal processing, the _____ E_s of a continuous-time signal x

$$E_s = \langle x(t), x(t) \rangle = \int_{-\infty}^{\infty} |x(t)|^2 dt$$

_____ in this context is not, strictly speaking, the same as the conventional notion of _____ in physics and the other sciences. The two concepts are, however, closely related, and it is possible to convert from one to the other:

$$E = \frac{E_s}{Z} = \frac{1}{Z} \int_{-\infty}^{\infty} |x(t)|^2 dt$$

where Z represents the magnitude, in appropriate units of measure, of the load driven by the signal.

For example, if x

a. Audio signal processing   b. Emphasis
c. Essential bandwidth   d. Energy

49.   In mathematics, a group G is called _____ if there is a subset S of G such that any element of G can be written in one and only one way as a product of finitely many elements of S and their inverses.

A related but different notion is a _____ abelian group.

_____ groups first arose in the study of hyperbolic geometry, as examples of Fuchsian groups.

a. Leibniz formula   b. Barycentric coordinates
c. Boolean algebra   d. Free

50.   In mathematics, an _____ is a vector space with the additional structure of inner product. This additional structure associates each pair of vectors in the space with a scalar quantity known as the inner product of the vectors. Inner products allow the rigorous introduction of intuitive geometrical notions such as the length of a vector or the angle between two vectors.

a. A chemical equation   b. A Mathematical Theory of Communication
c. A posteriori   d. Inner product space

51.   In trigonometry and geometry, _____ is the process of determining the location of a point by measuring angles to it from known points at either end of a fixed baseline, rather than measuring distances to the point directly. The point can then be fixed as the third point of a triangle with one known side and two known angles.

_____ can also refer to the accurate surveying of systems of very large triangles, called _____ networks.

a. 120-cell   b. 1-center problem
c. 2-3 heap   d. Triangulation

52.   _____ is a sparse matrix, whose non-zero entries are confined to a diagonal band, comprizing the main diagonal and zero or more diagonals on either side.

a. 2-3 heap   b. 1-center problem
c. 120-cell   d. Banded matrix

53. In mathematics, an _____ or member of a set is any one of the distinct objects that make up that set.

Writing A = {1,2,3,4}, means that the _____s of the set A are the numbers 1, 2, 3 and 4. Groups of _____s of A, for example {1,2}, are subsets of A.

a. Universal code   b. Ideal
c. Order   d. Element

54. In mathematics, a _____ is a rectangular table of elements, which may be numbers or, more generally, any abstract quantities that can be added and multiplied. Matrices are used to describe linear equations, keep track of the coefficients of linear transformations and to record data that depend on multiple parameters. Matrices are described by the field of _____ theory.

a. Matrix   b. Coherent
c. Double counting   d. Compression

55. A _____, from the French patron, is a type of theme of recurring events of or objects, sometimes referred to as elements of a set. These elements repeat in a predictable manner. It can be a template or model which can be used to generate things or parts of a thing, especially if the things that are created have enough in common for the underlying _____ to be inferred, in which case the things are said to exhibit the unique _____.

a. 1-center problem   b. Pattern
c. 2-3 heap   d. 120-cell

56. In the mathematical subfield of numerical analysis a _____ is a matrix populated primarily with zeros.

Conceptually, sparsity corresponds to systems which are loosely coupled. Consider a line of balls connected by springs from one to the next; this is a sparse system.

a. Pigeonhole principle   b. Binomial coefficient
c. Macdonald polynomials   d. Sparse matrix

57. In the mathematical subfield of numerical analysis a sparse matrix is a matrix populated primarily with zeros.

Conceptually, _____ corresponds to systems which are loosely coupled. Consider a line of balls connected by springs from one to the next; this is a sparse system.

a. Dyson conjecture   b. Bell polynomial
c. Sparsity   d. Twelvefold way

1.   A _____ is an efficient algorithm to compute the discrete Fourier transform and its inverse

A DFT decomposes a sequence of values into components of different frequencies.

a. 120-cell

b. 1-center problem

c. Fast Fourier transform

d. 2-3 heap

2.   The requirement that L have strictly positive diagonal entries can be dropped to extend the factorization to the positive semidefinite case. The statement then reads: a square matrix A has a Cholesky decomposition if and only if A is Hermitian and positive semi-definite. _____ for positive semidefinite matrices are not unique in general.

a. Wold decomposition

b. Singular values

c. Positive definite kernel

d. Cholesky factorizations

3.   In mathematics, the _____ s are an extension of the real numbers obtained by adjoining an imaginary unit, denoted i, which satisfies:

$$i^2 = -1.$$

Every _____ can be written in the form a + bi, where a and b are real numbers called the real part and the imaginary part of the _____, respectively.

_____ s are a field, and thus have addition, subtraction, multiplication, and division operations. These operations extend the corresponding operations on real numbers, although with a number of additional elegant and useful properties, e.g., negative real numbers can be obtained by squaring _____ s.

a. Real part

b. 1-center problem

c. 120-cell

d. Complex number

4.   In mathematics and in the sciences, a _____ (plural: _____ e, formulæ or _____ s) is a concise way of expressing information symbolically (as in a mathematical or chemical _____), or a general relationship between quantities. One of many famous _____ e is Albert Einstein's E = mc^2 (see special relativity

In mathematics, a _____ is a key to solve an equation with variables. For example, the problem of determining the volume of a sphere is one that requires a significant amount of integral calculus to solve.

a. 1-center problem

b. 120-cell

c. 2-3 heap

d. Formula

5.   In mathematics, a _____ is a vector space of functions equipped with a norm that is a combination of L^p norms of the function itself as well as its derivatives up to a given order. The derivatives are understood in a suitable weak sense to make the space complete, thus a Banach space. Intuitively, a _____ is a Banach space or Hilbert space of functions with sufficiently many derivatives for some application domain, such as partial differential equations, and equipped with a norm that measures both the size and smoothness of a function.

a. 120-cell

b. 1-center problem

c. 2-3 heap

d. Sobolev space

6. In mathematics, a _____ decomposes a periodic function into a sum of simple oscillating functions, namely sines and cosines. The study of _____ is a branch of Fourier analysis. _____ were introduced by Joseph Fourier for the purpose of solving the heat equation in a metal plate.

   a. Fourier series of a periodic function converges   b. Triangle wave
   c. 1-center problem   d. Fourier series

7. In mathematics, a _____ is a constant multiplicative factor of a certain object. For example, in the expression $9x^2$, the _____ of x^2 is 9.

The object can be such things as a variable, a vector, a function, etc.

   a. Multivariate division algorithm   b. Coefficient
   c. Fibonacci polynomials   d. Stability radius

8. In linear algebra and functional analysis, a _____ is a linear transformation P from a vector space to itself such that $P^2 = P$. It leaves its image unchanged. Though abstract, this definition of '_____' formalizes and generalizes the idea of graphical _____.

   a. Deviance   b. Critical point
   c. Characteristic function   d. Projection

9. In mathematics, a _____ is often represented as the sum of a sequence of terms. That is, a _____ is represented as a list of numbers with addition operations between them, for example this arithmetic sequence:

     1 + 2 + 3 + 4 + 5 + ... + 99 + 100

In most cases of interest the terms of the sequence are produced according to a certain rule, such as by a formula, by an algorithm, by a sequence of measurements, or even by a random number generator.

   a. Concavity   b. Contact
   c. Blind   d. Series

10. In mathematics, a _____ is a statement that can be proved on the basis of explicitly stated or previously agreed assumptions.

   a. Boolean function   b. Disjunction introduction
   c. Theorem   d. Logical value

11. In mathematics, the trapezium rule or _____ is a way to approximately calculate the definite integral

$$\int_a^b f(x)\, dx.$$

The trapezium rule works by approximating the region under the graph of the function f by a trapezium and calculating its area. It follows that

$$\int_a^b f(x)\, dx \approx (b-a)\frac{f(a)+f(b)}{2}.$$

To calculate this integral more accurately, one first splits the interval of integration [a,b] into n smaller subintervals, and then applies the trapezium rule on each of them. One obtains the composite trapezium rule:

$$\int_a^b f(x)\, dx \approx \frac{b-a}{n}\left[\frac{f(a)+f(b)}{2} + \sum_{k=1}^{n-1} f\left(a + k\frac{b-a}{n}\right)\right].$$

This can alternatively be written as:

$$\int_a^b f(x)\, dx \approx \frac{b-a}{2n}\left(f(x_0) + 2f(x_1) + 2f(x_2) + \cdots + 2f(x_{n-1}) + f(x_n)\right)$$

where

$$x_k = a + k\frac{b-a}{n}, \text{ for } k = 0, 1, \ldots, n.$$

a. 2-3 heap   b. 120-cell

c. 1-center problem   d. Trapezoidal rule

12. In mathematical analysis, the _____ is the collection of functions

$$D_n(x) = \sum_{k=-n}^{n} e^{ikx} = 1 + 2\sum_{k=1}^{n} \cos(kx) = \frac{\sin\left(\left(n+\frac{1}{2}\right)x\right)}{\sin(x/2)}.$$

It is named after Johann Peter Gustav Lejeune Dirichlet.

The importance of the _____ comes from its relation to Fourier series. The convolution of $D_n\pi$ is the nth-degree Fourier series approximation to f.

a. Dirichlet kernel   b. Mountain pass theorem

c. Constructive analysis   d. Total variation

13. In mathematics, the _____ is one of the specific forms of Fourier analysis. It transforms one function into another, which is called the frequency domain representation, or simply the DFT, of the original function. But the DFT requires an input function that is discrete and whose non-zero values have a limited duration.

a. Discrete Fourier transform

b. S plane

c. Number-theoretic transform

d. Fourier analysis

14.   In mathematics, the _____ of a number n is the number that, when added to n, yields zero. The _____ of n is denoted −n. For example, 7 is −7, because 7 + (−7) = 0, and the _____ of −0.3 is 0.3, because −0.3 + 0.3 = 0.

a. Algebraic structure

b. Arity

c. Additive inverse

d. Associativity

15.   The _____ is given by

$$x_n = \frac{1}{N} \sum_{k=0}^{N-1} X_k e^{\frac{2\pi i}{N} kn} \qquad n = 0, \ldots, N - 1.$$

A simple description of these equations is that the complex numbers X_k represent the amplitude and phase of the different sinusoidal components of the input 'signal' x_n. The DFT computes the X_k from the x_n, while the _____ shows how to compute the x_n as a sum of sinusoidal components $(1/N) X_k e^{\frac{2\pi i}{N} kn}$ with frequency k / N cycles per sample. By writing the equations in this form, we are making extensive use of Euler's formula to express sinusoids in terms of complex exponentials, which are much easier to manipulate.

a. Inverse discrete Fourier transform

b. A posteriori

c. A Mathematical Theory of Communication

d. A chemical equation

16.   In the various branches of mathematics that fall under the heading of abstract algebra, the _____ of a homomorphism measures the degree to which the homomorphism fails to be injective. An important special case is the _____ of a matrix, also called the null space.

The definition of _____ takes various forms in various contexts.

a. Leibniz formula

b. Constructivism

c. Bertrand paradox

d. Kernel

17.   _____ is a method of constructing new data points from a discrete set of known data points.

a. Archimedes' use of infinitesimals

b. Uniform convergence

c. Integration by substitution

d. Interpolation

18.   In mathematics, the _____ functions are functions of an angle; they are important when studying triangles and modeling periodic phenomena, among many other applications.

a. Trigonometric

b. Gudermannian function

c. Coversine

d. Law of sines

19.   In mathematics, _____ is interpolation with trigonometric polynomials. Interpolation is the process of finding a function which goes through some given data points. For _____, this function has to be a trigonometric polynomial, that is, a sum of sines and cosines of given periods.

a. Simple rational approximation

b. Monotone cubic interpolation

c. Linear predictive analysis

d. Trigonometric interpolation

20. In mathematics, a _____ is a natural number which has exactly two distinct natural number divisors: 1 and itself. An infinitude of _____s exists, as demonstrated by Euclid around 300 BC. The first twenty-five _____s are:

2, 3, 5, 7, 11, 13, 17, 19, 23, 29, 31, 37, 41, 43, 47, 53, 59, 61, 67, 71, 73, 79, 83, 89, 97.

a. Pronic number

b. Highly composite number

c. Prime number

d. Perrin number

21. In mathematics, the _____ is a Fourier-related transform similar to the discrete Fourier transform, but using a purely real matrix. It is equivalent to the imaginary parts of a DFT of roughly twice the length, operating on real data with odd symmetry, where in some variants the input and/or output data are shifted by half a sample.

A related transform is the discrete cosine transform, which is equivalent to a DFT of real and even functions.

a. Quantum Fourier transform

b. Legendre transform

c. Chirplet transform

d. Discrete sine transform

22. The _____ of an angle is the ratio of the length of the opposite side to the length of the hypotenuse. In our case

$$\sin A = \frac{\text{opposite}}{\text{hypotenuse}} = \frac{a}{h}.$$

Note that this ratio does not depend on size of the particular right triangle chosen, as long as it contains the angle A, since all such triangles are similar.

The cosine of an angle is the ratio of the length of the adjacent side to the length of the hypotenuse.

a. Sine

b. Law of sines

c. Right angle

d. Trigonometric functions

23. A _____ expresses a sequence of finitely many data points in terms of a sum of cosine functions oscillating at different frequencies. DCTs are important to numerous applications in science and engineering, from lossy compression of audio and images, to spectral methods for the numerical solution of partial differential equations. The use of cosine rather than sine functions is critical in these applications: for compression, it turns out that cosine functions are much more efficient, whereas for differential equations the cosines express a particular choice of boundary conditions.

a. Recursive least squares

b. Sampling rate

c. Least-squares spectral analysis

d. Discrete cosine transform

24. The mathematical concept of a _____ expresses the intuitive idea of deterministic dependence between two quantities, one of which is viewed as primary and the other as secondary. A _____ then is a way to associate a unique output for each input of a specified type, for example, a real number or an element of a given set.

   a. Coherent   b. Going up
   c. Grill   d. Function

25.   In mathematics, even functions and _____s are functions which satisfy particular symmetry relations, with respect to taking additive inverses. They are important in many areas of mathematical analysis, especially the theory of power series and Fourier series. They are named for the parity of the powers of the power functions which satisfy each condition: the function f(x) = x^n is an even function if n is an even integer, and it is an _____ if n is an odd integer.
   a. A Mathematical Theory of Communication   b. A chemical equation
   c. A posteriori   d. Odd function

26.   In mathematics, a _____ is a function that repeats its values after some definite period has been added to its independent variable. This property is called periodicity. An illustration of a _____ with period P.

Everyday examples are seen when the variable is time; for instance the hands of a clock or the phases of the moon show periodic behaviour.

   a. Method of indivisibles   b. Calculus controversy
   c. Periodic function   d. Hyperbolic angle

27.   In mathematics, the qualifier _____ is used to indicate that a certain property is defined by considering each value f of some function f. An example is _____ convergence of functions -- a sequence of functions

$$\{f_n\}_{n=1}^{\infty}$$

with

$$f_n : X \longrightarrow Y$$

converges _____ to a function f if for each x in X

$$\lim_{n \to \infty} f_n(x) = f(x).$$

An important class of _____ concepts are the _____ operations -- operations defined on functions by applying the operations to function values separately for each point in the domain of definition. These include

_____ operations inherit such properties as associativity, commutativity and distributivity from corresponding operations on the codomain.

An example of an operation on functions which is not _____ is convolution.

   a. Concurrent lines   b. Pointwise
   c. Percentage points   d. LHS

28. In mathematics, _____ is one of various senses in which a sequence of functions can converge to a particular function.

Suppose $\{\,f_n\,\}$ is a sequence of functions sharing the same domain in common. Consider the statement

$$\lim_{n\to\infty} f_n(x) = f(x).$$

To say that this is true of each value of x in the domain, separately, is to say that the sequence $\{\,f_n\,\}$ converges pointwise to f, and often one writes

$$\lim_{n\to\infty} f_n(x) = f(x) \ \text{pointwise}.$$

This concept is often contrasted with uniform convergence.

a. Real projective line
c. Gibbs phenomenon

b. Pinsky phenomenon
d. Pointwise convergence

29. A _____ is a set of standard clothing worn by members of an organization while participating in that organization's activity. Modern _____s are worn by armed forces and paramilitary organisations such as police, emergency services, security guards, in some workplaces and schools and by inmates in prisons. In some countries, some other officials also wear _____s in some of their duties; such is the case of the Commissioned Corps of the United States Public Health Service or the French prefects.

a. A chemical equation
c. A Mathematical Theory of Communication

b. A posteriori
d. Uniform

30. In the mathematical field of analysis, _____ is a type of convergence stronger than pointwise convergence. A sequence $\{\,f_n\,\}$ of functions converges uniformly to a limiting function f if the speed of convergence of f_n

The concept is important because several properties of the functions f_n, such as continuity and Riemann integrability, are transferred to the limit f if the convergence is uniform.

a. Archimedes' use of infinitesimals
c. Integration by substitution

b. Uniform convergence
d. Infinite series

31. In mathematics and, in particular, functional analysis, _____ is a mathematical operation on two functions f and g, producing a third function that is typically viewed as a modified version of one of the original functions. _____ is similar to cross-correlation. It has applications that include statistics, computer vision, image and signal processing, electrical engineering, and differential equations.

a. Coordinate-free
c. Convolution

b. Cook reduction
d. Beth numbers

32. In vector calculus, the _____ is shorthand for either the _____ matrix or its determinant, the _____ determinant.

In algebraic geometry the _____ of a curve means the _____ variety: a group variety associated to the curve, in which the curve can be embedded.

These concepts are all named after the mathematician Carl Gustav Jacob Jacobi.

a. Monkey saddle   b. Shift theorem
c. Surface integral   d. Jacobian

33.   In probability theory, a probability distribution is called _____ if its cumulative distribution function is _____.
That is equivalent to saying that for random variables X with the distribution in question, Pr[X = a] = 0 for all real numbers a. If the distribution of X is _____ then X is called a _____ random variable.
a. Continuous phase modulation   b. Conull set
c. Concatenated codes   d. Continuous

34.   Continuous functions are of utmost importance in mathematics and applications. However, not all functions are continuous. If a function is not continuous at a point in its domain, one says that it has a _____ there. The set of all points of _____ of a function may be a discrete set, a dense set, or even the entire domain of the function.
a. Core   b. Cusp
c. Discontinuity   d. Derivation

35.   Then, the point x_0 = 1 is a _____. The function in example 3, an essential discontinuity

3. Consider the function

$$f(x) = \begin{cases} \sin \frac{5}{x-1} & \text{for } x < 1 \\ 0 & \text{for } x = 1 \\ \frac{0.1}{x-1} & \text{for } x > 1 \end{cases}$$

Then, the point x_0 = 1 is an essential discontinuity.

a. 1-center problem   b. 120-cell
c. 2-3 heap   d. Jump discontinuity

36.   In mathematics, a _____ is a rectangular table of elements, which may be numbers or, more generally, any abstract quantities that can be added and multiplied. Matrices are used to describe linear equations, keep track of the coefficients of linear transformations and to record data that depend on multiple parameters. Matrices are described by the field of _____ theory.
a. Compression   b. Coherent
c. Double counting   d. Matrix

37.   The word piecewise is also used to describe any property of a piecewise-defined function that holds for each piece but may not hold for the whole domain of the function. A function is _____ or piecewise continuously differentiable if each piece is differentiable throughout its domain. In convex analysis, the notion of a derivative may be replaced by that of the subderivative for piecewise functions.
   a. High-dimensional model representation
   c. Linear map
   b. Tetraview
   d. Piecewise differentiable

38.   In mathematics, the _____ or Pythagoras' theorem is a relation in Euclidean geometry among the three sides of a right triangle. The theorem is named after the Greek mathematician Pythagoras, who by tradition is credited with its discovery and proof, although it is often argued that knowledge of the theory predates him.. The theorem is as follows:

In any right triangle, the area of the square whose side is the hypotenuse is equal to the sum of the areas of the squares whose sides are the two legs.

   a. 1-center problem
   c. 2-3 heap
   b. 120-cell
   d. Pythagorean theorem

39.   In mathematics, an _____ is a statement about the relative size or order of two objects, or about whether they are the same or not

   ● The notation a < b means that a is less than b.
   ● The notation a > b means that a is greater than b.
   ● The notation a ≠ b means that a is not equal to b, but does not say that one is bigger than the other or even that they can be compared in size.

In all these cases, a is not equal to b, hence, '_____'.

These relations are known as strict _____

   ● The notation a ≤ b means that a is less than or equal to b;
   ● The notation a ≥ b means that a is greater than or equal to b;

An additional use of the notation is to show that one quantity is much greater than another, normally by several orders of magnitude.

   ● The notation a << b means that a is much less than b.
   ● The notation a >> b means that a is much greater than b.

If the sense of the _____ is the same for all values of the variables for which its members are defined, then the _____ is called an 'absolute' or 'unconditional' _____. If the sense of an _____ holds only for certain values of the variables involved, but is reversed or destroyed for other values of the variables, it is called a conditional _____.

An _____ may appear unsolvable because it only states whether a number is larger or smaller than another number; but it is possible to apply the same operations for equalities to inequalities. For example, to find x for the _____ 10x > 23 one would divide 23 by 10.

  a. Inequality   b. A posteriori
  c. A Mathematical Theory of Communication   d. A chemical equation

40. In statistics, _____ has two related meanings:

- the arithmetic _____.
- the expected value of a random variable, which is also called the population _____.

It is sometimes stated that the '_____' _____s average. This is incorrect if '_____' is taken in the specific sense of 'arithmetic _____' as there are different types of averages: the _____, median, and mode. For instance, average house prices almost always use the median value for the average.

For a real-valued random variable X, the _____ is the expectation of X.

  a. Statistical population   b. Probability
  c. Proportional hazards model   d. Mean

41. In calculus, the _____ states, roughly, that given a section of a smooth curve, there is at least one point on that section at which the derivative of the curve is equal to the 'average' derivative of the section. It is used to prove theorems that make global conclusions about a function on an interval starting from local hypotheses about derivatives at points of the interval.

This theorem can be understood concretely by applying it to motion: if a car travels one hundred miles in one hour, so that its average speed during that time was 100 miles per hour, then at some time its instantaneous speed must have been exactly 100 miles per hour.

  a. Fundamental Theorem of Calculus   b. Mean value theorem
  c. Calculus controversy   d. Functional integration

42. A _____ is a kind of non-sinusoidal waveform, most typically encountered in electronics and signal processing. An ideal _____ alternates regularly and instantaneously between two levels.

_____s are universally encountered in digital switching circuits and are naturally generated by binary logic devices.

  a. Sawtooth wave   b. Signal compression
  c. Resonance   d. Square wave

43. The _____ , is achieved in a packed stadium when successive groups of spectators briefly stand and raise their arms. Each spectator is required to rise at the same time as those straight in front and behind, and slightly after the person immediately to either the right or the left. Immediately upon stretching to full height, the spectator returns to the usual seated position.

   a. Pauli exclusion principle   b. Thermodynamic limit

   c. Lagrangian   d. Wave

44. In mathematics, a _____ is a function for which, intuitively, small changes in the input result in small changes in the output. Otherwise, a function is said to be discontinuous. A _____ with a continuous inverse function is called bicontinuous.

   a. Charles's Law   b. Beth numbers

   c. Contraction mapping   d. Continuous function

45. Georg Friedrich Bernhard _____ was a German mathematician who made important contributions to analysis and differential geometry, some of them paving the way for the later development of general relativity.

_____ was born in Breselenz, a village near Dannenberg in the Kingdom of Hanover in what is today Germany. His father, Friedrich Bernhard _____, was a poor Lutheran pastor in Breselenz who fought in the Napoleonic Wars.

   a. Gustave Bertrand   b. Paul C. van Oorschot

   c. Brook Taylor   d. Riemann

46. In the branch of mathematics known as real analysis, the _____, created by Bernhard Riemann, was the first rigorous definition of the integral of a function on an interval. While the _____ is unsuitable for many theoretical purposes, it is one of the easiest integrals to define. Some of these technical deficiencies can be remedied by the Riemann-Stieltjes integral, and most of them disappear in the Lebesgue integral.

   a. Darboux integral   b. Skorokhod integral

   c. Russo-Vallois integral   d. Riemann integral

47. In commutative algebra, the notions of an element _____ over a ring, and of an _____ extension of rings, are a generalization of the notions in field theory of an element being algebraic over a field, and of an algebraic extension of fields.

The special case of greatest interest in number theory is that of complex numbers _____ over the ring of integers Z.

The term ring will be understood to mean commutative ring with a unit.

   a. Integral   b. Integral test for convergence

   c. Arc length   d. Antidifferentiation

48. In mathematics, _____s are well-behaved functions between measurable spaces. Functions studied in analysis that are not measurable are generally considered pathological.

If Σ is a σ-algebra over a set X and T is a σ-algebra over Y, then a function f : X → Y is measurable Σ/T if the preimage of every set in T is in Σ.

a. Nikodym set
c. Cantor set

b. Borel-Cantelli lemma
d. Measurable function

49.   In mathematics the concept of a _____ generalizes notions such as 'length', 'area', and 'volume'. Informally, given some base set, a '_____' is any consistent assignment of 'sizes' to the subsets of the base set. Depending on the application, the 'size' of a subset may be interpreted as its physical size, the amount of something that lies within the subset, or the probability that some random process will yield a result within the subset.

a. Congruent
c. Lattice

b. Measure
d. Cusp

50.   In mathematical analysis, a metric space M is said to be _____ (or Cauchy) if every Cauchy sequence of points in M has a limit that is also in M or alternatively if every Cauchy sequence in M converges in M.

Intuitively, a space is _____ if there are no 'points missing' from it (inside or at the boundary.) For instance, the set of rational numbers is not _____, because $\sqrt{2}$ is 'missing' from it, even though one can construct a Cauchy sequence of rational numbers that converges to it.

a. 1-center problem
c. Complete

b. 2-3 heap
d. 120-cell

51.   In mathematics, two vectors are _____ if they are perpendicular. For example, a subway and the street above, although they do not physically intersect, are _____ if they cross at a right angle.

a. Algebraic structure
c. Unique factorization domain

b. Additive identity
d. Orthogonal

52.   In mathematics, a _____, named after Augustin Cauchy, is a sequence whose elements become arbitrarily close to each other as the sequence progresses. To be more precise, by dropping enough terms from the start of the sequence, it is possible to make the maximum of the distances from any of the remaining elements to any other such element smaller than any preassigned positive value.

In other words, suppose a pre-assigned positive real value ε is chosen.

a. Hausdorff distance
c. Contraction mapping

b. Cauchy sequence
d. Systolic inequalities for curves on surfaces

53.   In mathematics, with 2- or 3-dimensional vectors with real-valued entries, the idea of the 'length' of a vector is intuitive and can easily be extended to any real vector space R^n. It turns out that the following properties of 'vector length' are the crucial ones.

1.   The zero vector, 0, has zero length; every other vector has a positive length.
2.   Multiplying a vector by a positive number changes its length without changing its direction. See unit vector.
3.   The triangle inequality holds. That is, taking norms as distances, the distance from point A through B to C is never shorter than going directly from A to C, or the shortest distance between any two points is a straight line.

Their generalization for more abstract vector spaces, leads to the notion of norm. A vector space on which a norm is defined is then called a _____.

a. 1-center problem   b. 2-3 heap
c. 120-cell   d. Normed vector space

54.   In physics and in _____ calculus, a _____ is a concept characterized by a magnitude and a direction. A _____ can be thought of as an arrow in Euclidean space, drawn from an initial point A pointing to a terminal point B.
a. Deviation   b. Constraint
c. Dominance   d. Vector

55.   In mathematics, a _____ is a collection of objects called vectors that may be scaled and added. These two operations must adhere to a number of axioms that generalize common properties of tuples of real numbers such as vectors in the plane or three-dimensional Euclidean space. _____s are a keystone of linear algebra, and much of their theory is of a linear nature.
a. Geodesic   b. Minkowski space
c. Moment of inertia   d. Vector space

1.   In mathematics, a _____ is a vector space of functions equipped with a norm that is a combination of L^P norms of the function itself as well as its derivatives up to a given order. The derivatives are understood in a suitable weak sense to make the space complete, thus a Banach space. Intuitively, a _____ is a Banach space or Hilbert space of functions with sufficiently many derivatives for some application domain, such as partial differential equations, and equipped with a norm that measures both the size and smoothness of a function.

   a. Sobolev space   b. 1-center problem
   c. 120-cell   d. 2-3 heap

2.   _____ is a general term for any type of information processing. This includes phenomena ranging from human thinking to calculations with a more narrow meaning. _____ is a process following a well-defined model that is understood and can be expressed in an algorithm, protocol, network topology, etc.

   a. Computation   b. 2-3 heap
   c. 1-center problem   d. 120-cell

3.   In mathematics, computing, linguistics and related subjects, an _____ is a sequence of finite instructions, often used for calculation and data processing. It is formally a type of effective method in which a list of well-defined instructions for completing a task will, when given an initial state, proceed through a well-defined series of successive states, eventually terminating in an end-state. The transition from one state to the next is not necessarily deterministic; some _____s, known as probabilistic _____s, incorporate randomness.

   a. Out-of-core   b. In-place algorithm
   c. Approximate counting algorithm   d. Algorithm

4.   _____ is usually defined as the activity of using and developing computer technology, computer hardware and software. It is the computer-specific part of information technology. Computer science (or _____ science) is the study and the science of the theoretical foundations of information and computation and their implementation and application in computer systems.

   a. Computing   b. Parallel Random Access Machine
   c. Deterministic finite state machine   d. Probabilistic Turing Machine

5.   The requirement that L have strictly positive diagonal entries can be dropped to extend the factorization to the positive semidefinite case. The statement then reads: a square matrix A has a Cholesky decomposition if and only if A is Hermitian and positive semi-definite. _____ for positive semidefinite matrices are not unique in general.

   a. Singular values   b. Positive definite kernel
   c. Wold decomposition   d. Cholesky factorizations

6.   A _____ in computer science is a way of storing data in a computer so that it can be used efficiently. It is an organization of mathematical and logical concepts of data. Often a carefully chosen _____ will allow the most efficient algorithm to be used.

   a. Data structure   b. BK-tree
   c. Spaghetti stack   d. Self-organizing list

7.   In commutative algebra, the notions of an element _____ over a ring, and of an _____ extension of rings, are a generalization of the notions in field theory of an element being algebraic over a field, and of an algebraic extension of fields.

The special case of greatest interest in number theory is that of complex numbers _____ over the ring of integers Z.

The term ring will be understood to mean commutative ring with a unit.

a. Integral   b. Antidifferentiation
c. Integral test for convergence   d. Arc length

8. In trigonometry and geometry, _____ is the process of determining the location of a point by measuring angles to it from known points at either end of a fixed baseline, rather than measuring distances to the point directly. The point can then be fixed as the third point of a triangle with one known side and two known angles.

_____ can also refer to the accurate surveying of systems of very large triangles, called _____ networks.

a. 120-cell   b. 1-center problem
c. 2-3 heap   d. Triangulation

9. In mathematics, the _____ or Pythagoras' theorem is a relation in Euclidean geometry among the three sides of a right triangle. The theorem is named after the Greek mathematician Pythagoras, who by tradition is credited with its discovery and proof, although it is often argued that knowledge of the theory predates him.. The theorem is as follows:

In any right triangle, the area of the square whose side is the hypotenuse is equal to the sum of the areas of the squares whose sides are the two legs.

a. 1-center problem   b. 2-3 heap
c. 120-cell   d. Pythagorean theorem

10. In mathematics and in the sciences, a _____ (plural: _____e, formulæ or _____s) is a concise way of expressing information symbolically (as in a mathematical or chemical _____), or a general relationship between quantities. One of many famous _____e is Albert Einstein's $E = mc^2$ (see special relativity

In mathematics, a _____ is a key to solve an equation with variables. For example, the problem of determining the volume of a sphere is one that requires a significant amount of integral calculus to solve.

a. 120-cell   b. Formula
c. 2-3 heap   d. 1-center problem

11. Chemical formula used for a series of compounds that differ from each other by a constant unit is called _____. Such a series is called the homologous series, while its members are called homologs.

The Hill system is a system of writing chemical formulas such that the number of carbon atoms in a molecule is indicated first, the number of hydrogen atoms next, and then the number of all other chemical elements subsequently, in alphabetical order.

a. 1-center problem   b. 2-3 heap
c. General formula   d. 120-cell

12. In mathematics, a _____ is a statement that can be proved on the basis of explicitly stated or previously agreed assumptions.
  a. Boolean function   b. Disjunction introduction
  c. Theorem   d. Logical value

13. A _____ is one of the basic shapes of geometry: a polygon with three corners or vertices and three sides or edges which are line segments. A _____ with vertices A, B, and C is denoted ABC.

In Euclidean geometry any three non-collinear points determine a unique _____ and a unique plane.

  a. 1-center problem   b. Fuhrmann circle
  c. Kepler triangle   d. Triangle

14. In vector calculus, the _____ is shorthand for either the _____ matrix or its determinant, the _____ determinant.

In algebraic geometry the _____ of a curve means the _____ variety: a group variety associated to the curve, in which the curve can be embedded.

These concepts are all named after the mathematician Carl Gustav Jacob Jacobi.

  a. Shift theorem   b. Jacobian
  c. Monkey saddle   d. Surface integral

15. In mathematics, a _____ is a basic technique used to simplify problems in which the original variables are replaced with new ones; the new and old variables being related in some specified way. The intent is that the problem expressed in new variables may be simpler, or else equivalent to a better understood problem.

A very simple example of a useful variable change can be seen in the problem of finding the roots of the eighth order polynomial:

$$x^8 + 3x^4 + 2 = 0$$

Eighth order polynomial equations are generally impossible to solve in terms of elementary functions.

  a. Change of variables   b. Continuous wavelet
  c. Convergence of measures   d. Coordinate-free

16. In mathematics, a _____ is a rectangular table of elements, which may be numbers or, more generally, any abstract quantities that can be added and multiplied. Matrices are used to describe linear equations, keep track of the coefficients of linear transformations and to record data that depend on multiple parameters. Matrices are described by the field of _____ theory.

a. Matrix
c. Coherent

b. Double counting
d. Compression

17.   The _____ is a type of definite integral extended to functions of more than one real variable, for example, $fz = x^2 + y^2$. The rectangular region at the bottom of the body is the domain of integration, while the surface is the graph of the two-variable function to be integrated.

Introduction

Just as the definite integral of a positive function of one variable represents the area of the region between the graph of the function and the x-axis, the double integral of a positive function of two variables represents the volume of the region between the surface defined by the function and the plane which contains its domain.

a. Multiple integral
c. Surface of revolution

b. Solid of revolution
d. Signed measure

18.   In the case of Gaussian elimination, it is best to choose a pivot element with large absolute value. This improves the numerical stability. In _____, the algorithm considers all entries in the column of the matrix that is currently being considered, picks the entry with largest absolute value, and finally swaps rows such that this entry is the pivot in question.

a. 2-3 heap
c. 120-cell

b. 1-center problem
d. Partial pivoting

19.   In the mathematical subfield of numerical analysis a _____ is a matrix populated primarily with zeros.

Conceptually, sparsity corresponds to systems which are loosely coupled. Consider a line of balls connected by springs from one to the next; this is a sparse system.

a. Pigeonhole principle
c. Macdonald polynomials

b. Binomial coefficient
d. Sparse matrix

20.   In linear algebra, _____ is an efficient algorithm for solving systems of linear equations, finding the rank of a matrix, and calculating the inverse of an invertible square matrix. _____ is named after German mathematician and scientist Carl Friedrich Gauss.

Elementary row operations are used to reduce a matrix to row echelon form.

a. Crout matrix decomposition
c. Cholesky decomposition

b. Conjugate gradient method
d. Gaussian elimination

21.   The process of solving a linear system of equations that has been transformed into row-echelon form or reduced row-echelon form is _____. The last equation is solved first, then the next-to-last, and so.

a. Crout matrix decomposition
c. Back substitution

b. Jacobi rotation
d. LU decomposition

22.   Pseudocode is a compact and informal high-level description of a computer programming algorithm that uses the structural conventions of some programming language, but is intended for human reading rather than machine reading. _____ typically omits details that are not essential for human understanding of the algorithm, such as variable declarations, system-specific code and subroutines. The programming language is augmented with natural language descriptions of the details, where convenient, or with compact mathematical notation.

  a. 120-cell   b. Pseudo-code

  c. Strand sort   d. 1-center problem

23.   _____ is a sparse matrix, whose non-zero entries are confined to a diagonal band, comprizing the main diagonal and zero or more diagonals on either side.

  a. Banded matrix   b. 120-cell

  c. 1-center problem   d. 2-3 heap

24.   The _____ of a matrix are those entries which change from an initial zero to a non-zero value during the execution of an algorithm. To reduce the memory requirements and the number of arithmetic operations used during an algorithm it is useful to minimize the _____ by switching rows and columns in the matrix. The symbolic Cholesky decomposition can be used to calculate the worst possible _____ before doing the actual Cholesky decomposition.

  a. Stanley-Wilf conjecture   b. Twelvefold way

  c. Graph transformation   d. Fill-in

25.   A _____, from the French patron, is a type of theme of recurring events of or objects, sometimes referred to as elements of a set. These elements repeat in a predictable manner. It can be a template or model which can be used to generate things or parts of a thing, especially if the things that are created have enough in common for the underlying _____ to be inferred, in which case the things are said to exhibit the unique _____.

  a. Pattern   b. 2-3 heap

  c. 1-center problem   d. 120-cell

26.   In the mathematical subfield of numerical analysis a sparse matrix is a matrix populated primarily with zeros.

Conceptually, _____ corresponds to systems which are loosely coupled. Consider a line of balls connected by springs from one to the next; this is a sparse system.

  a. Dyson conjecture   b. Twelvefold way

  c. Bell polynomial   d. Sparsity

27.   In computational mathematics, an _____ attempts to solve a problem (for example an equation or system of equations) by finding successive approximations to the solution starting from an initial guess. This approach is in contrast to direct methods, which attempt to solve the problem by a finite sequence of operations, and, in the absence of rounding errors, would deliver an exact solution (like solving a linear system of equations Ax = b by Gaussian elimination.) _____s are usually the only choice for nonlinear equations.

  a. A Mathematical Theory of Communication   b. A chemical equation

  c. A posteriori   d. Iterative method

28. A _____ is a mathematical model of a system based on the use of a linear operator. _____s typically exhibit features and properties that are much simpler than the general, nonlinear case. As a mathematical abstraction or idealization, _____s find important applications in automatic control theory, signal processing, and telecommunications.

   a. Hybrid system   b. Percolation
   c. Predispositioning Theory   d. Linear system

29. In mathematics, the idea of _____ has come to stand for a very general idea, extending the intuitive idea of 'gluing' in topology. Since the topologists' glue is actually the use of equivalence relations on topological spaces, the theory starts with some ideas on identification.

A sophisticated theory resulted.

   a. Deviance   b. Block size
   c. Dominance   d. Descent

30. In optimization, a _____ is a vector $\mathbf{p} \in \mathbb{R}^n$ that, in the sense below, moves us closer towards a local minimum $\mathbf{x}^*$ of our objective function $f : \mathbb{R}^n \to \mathbb{R}$.

Suppose we are computing $\mathbf{x}^*$ by an iterative method, such as linesearch. We define a _____ $\mathbf{p}_k \in \mathbb{R}^n$ at the kth iterate to be any $\mathbf{p}_k$ such that $\langle \mathbf{p}_k, \nabla f(\mathbf{x}_k) \rangle < 0$, where $\langle, \rangle$ denotes the inner product.

   a. Geometric programming   b. Complementarity problem
   c. Shekel function   d. Descent direction

31. In optimization, the _____ strategy is one of two basic iterative approaches to finding a local minimum $\mathbf{x}^*$ of an objective function $f : \mathbb{R}^n \to \mathbb{R}$. The other method is that of trust regions.

1. Set iteration counter $k = 0$, and make an initial guess, $\mathbf{x}_0$ for the minimum
2. Repeat:
3. Compute a descent direction $\mathbf{p}_k$
4. Choose α_k to 'loosely' minimize $\phi(\alpha) = f(\mathbf{x}_k + \alpha \mathbf{p}_k)$ over $\alpha \in \mathbb{R}$
5. Update $\mathbf{x}_{k+1} = \mathbf{x}_k + \alpha_k \mathbf{p}_k$, $k = k + 1$
6. Until $\| \nabla f(\mathbf{x}_k) \| <$ tolerance

In step 4 we can either exactly minimize ϕ, by solving $\phi'(\alpha_k) = 0$, or loosely, by asking for a sufficient decrease in ϕ. The latter may be performed in a number of ways, perhaps by doing a backtracking _____ or using the Wolfe conditions.

   a. Semidefinite programming   b. Moving least squares
   c. Least absolute deviations   d. Line search

32.   In algebra, a _____ of an element in a quadratic extension field of a field K is its image under the unique non-identity automorphism of the extended field that fixes K. If the extension is generated by a square root of an element r of K, then the _____ of $a + b\sqrt{r}$ is $a - b\sqrt{r}$ for $a, b \in K$, and in particular in the case of the field C of complex numbers as an extension of the field R of real numbers, the complex _____ of a + bi is a − bi.

Forming the sum or product of any element of the extension field with its _____ always gives an element of K.

   a. Trinomial   b. Real structure
   c. Conjugate   d. Relation algebra

33.   In vector calculus, the _____ of a scalar field is a vector field which points in the direction of the greatest rate of increase of the scalar field, and whose magnitude is the greatest rate of change.

A generalization of the _____ for functions on a Euclidean space which have values in another Euclidean space is the Jacobian. A further generalization for a function from one Banach space to another is the Fréchet derivative.

   a. Stationary point   b. Metric derivative
   c. Directional derivative   d. Gradient

34.   _____ is a core concept of basic mathematics, specifically in the fields of infinitesimal calculus and mathematical analysis. Given a function f

$$\int_a^b f(x)\, dx\,,$$

is equal to the area of a region in the xy-plane bounded by the graph of f, the x-axis, and the vertical lines x = a and x = b, with areas below the x-axis being subtracted.

The term 'integral' may also refer to the notion of antiderivative, a function F whose derivative is the given function f.

   a. Apex   b. OMAC
   c. Epigraph   d. Integration

35.   In calculus, and more generally in mathematical analysis, _____ is a rule that transforms the integral of products of functions into other, hopefully simpler, integrals. The rule arises from the product rule of differentiation.

If u = f[x], v = g[x], and the differentials du = f '[x] dx and dv = g'[x] dx; then in its simplest form the product rule is:

a. Integral test for convergence   b. Arc length
c. Integration by parts operator   d. Integration by parts

36.   There are several well-known theorems in functional analysis known as the _____. They are named in honour of Frigyes Riesz.

This theorem establishes an important connection between a Hilbert space and its dual space: if the underlying field is the real numbers, the two are isometrically isomorphic; if the field is the complex numbers, the two are isometrically anti-isomorphic.

a. Continuously embedded   b. Riesz representation theorem
c. Conjugate indices   d. Compact convergence

37.   In general, an object is complete if nothing needs to be added to it. This notion is made more specific in various fields.

In logic, semantic _____ is the converse of soundness for formal systems.

a. Giuseppe Peano   b. Set theory
c. Logical equality   d. Completeness

38.   _____ is a fundamental construction of differential calculus and admits many possible generalizations within the fields of mathematical analysis, combinatorics, algebra, and geometry.

In real, complex, and functional analysis, _____s are generalized to functions of several real or complex variables and functions between topological vector spaces. An important case is the variational _____ in the calculus of variations.

a. Derivative   b. Lin-Tsien equation
c. Functional derivative   d. Metric derivative

39.   In mathematics, a _____ of a function of several variables is its derivative with respect to one of those variables with the others held constant. _____s are useful in vector calculus and differential geometry.

The _____ of a function f with respect to the variable x is written as f_x, $\partial_x f$, or $\partial f/\partial x$.

a. Laplacian   b. Critical number
c. Laplace invariant   d. Partial derivative

40.   In linear algebra, the _____ of an n-by-n square matrix A is defined to be the sum of the elements on the main diagonal of A. wikimedia.org/math/8/2/b/82be32fa00bd97ebbc066aec3dfe72da.png">

where a_{ij} represents the entry on the ith row and jth column of A. Equivalently, the _____ of a matrix is the sum of its eigenvalues, making it an invariant with respect to a change of basis.

a. Blinding   b. Lattice
c. Trace   d. Constructivism

41.   In mathematics, the concept of _____ plays an important role in studying the existence and uniqueness of solutions to boundary value problems, that is, to partial differential equations with prescribed boundary conditions. The _____ makes it possible to extend the notion of restriction of a function to the boundary of its domain to 'generalized' functions in a Sobolev space.

Let Ω be a bounded open set in the Euclidean space $\mathbb{R}^n$ with C^1 boundary $\partial\Omega$. If u is a function that is C^1 (or even just continuous) on the closure $\overline{\Omega}$ of Ω, its function restriction is well-defined and continuous on $\partial\Omega$. If however, u is the solution to some partial differential equation, it is in general a weak solution, so it belongs to some Sobolev space.

a. 2-3 heap   b. 1-center problem
c. Trace operator   d. 120-cell

42.   In mathematics, a _____ is a generalization of the concept of the derivative of a function (strong derivative) for functions not assumed differentiable, but only integrable. See distributions for an even more general definition.

Let u be a function in the Lebesgue space $L^1([a,b])$.

a. Schwartz kernel theorem   b. Generalized functions
c. Logarithmically-spaced Dirac comb   d. Weak derivative

43.   In signal processing, the _____ E_s of a continuous-time signal x

$$E_s \;=\; \langle x(t), x(t) \rangle \;=\; \int_{-\infty}^{\infty} |x(t)|^2 dt$$

_____ in this context is not, strictly speaking, the same as the conventional notion of _____ in physics and the other sciences. The two concepts are, however, closely related, and it is possible to convert from one to the other:

$$E = \frac{E_s}{Z} = \frac{1}{Z} \int_{-\infty}^{\infty} |x(t)|^2 dt$$

where Z represents the magnitude, in appropriate units of measure, of the load driven by the signal.

For example, if x

a. Essential bandwidth
c. Energy

b. Audio signal processing
d. Emphasis

44.   In mathematics, an _____ is a statement about the relative size or order of two objects, or about whether they are the same or not

- The notation a < b means that a is less than b.
- The notation a > b means that a is greater than b.
- The notation a ≠ b means that a is not equal to b, but does not say that one is bigger than the other or even that they can be compared in size.

In all these cases, a is not equal to b, hence, '_____'.

These relations are known as strict _____

- The notation a ≤ b means that a is less than or equal to b;
- The notation a ≥ b means that a is greater than or equal to b;

An additional use of the notation is to show that one quantity is much greater than another, normally by several orders of magnitude.

- The notation a << b means that a is much less than b.
- The notation a >> b means that a is much greater than b.

If the sense of the _____ is the same for all values of the variables for which its members are defined, then the _____ is called an 'absolute' or 'unconditional' _____. If the sense of an _____ holds only for certain values of the variables involved, but is reversed or destroyed for other values of the variables, it is called a conditional _____.

An _____ may appear unsolvable because it only states whether a number is larger or smaller than another number; but it is possible to apply the same operations for equalities to inequalities. For example, to find x for the _____ 10x > 23 one would divide 23 by 10.

a. A posteriori   b. A Mathematical Theory of Communication
c. A chemical equation   d. Inequality

45.   In linear algebra, functional analysis and related areas of mathematics, a _____ is a function that assigns a strictly
positive length or size to all vectors in a vector space, other than the zero vector. A seminorm, on the other hand, is allowed to
assign zero length to some non-zero vectors.

A simple example is the 2-dimensional Euclidean space R^2 equipped with the Euclidean _____.

a. Norm   b. Leibniz formula
c. Going up   d. Compression

46.   A pair x_k, y_k is called a data point and f is called an _____ for the data points.

When the numbers y_k are given by a known function f, we sometimes write f_k.

For example, suppose we have a table like this, which gives some values of an unknown function f.

a. Interpolant   b. A Mathematical Theory of Communication
c. A chemical equation   d. A posteriori

47.   In mathematics, the _____, name after Ivar Fredholm, is one of Fredholm's theorems and is a result in Fredholm
theory. It may be expressed in several ways, as a theorem of linear algebra, a theorem of integral equations, or as a theorem on
Fredholm operators. Part of the result states that, a non-zero complex number in the spectrum of a compact operator is an
eigenvalue.
a. Fredholm operator   b. Liouville-Neumann series
c. Fredholm integral equation   d. Fredholm alternative

48.   In statistics the _____ of an event i is the number n_i of times the event occurred in the experiment or the study.
These frequencies are often graphically represented in histograms.

We speak of absolute frequencies, when the counts n_i themselves are given and of

$$f_i = \frac{n_i}{N} = \frac{n_i}{\sum_i n_i}$$

Taking the f_i for all i and tabulating or plotting them leads to a _____ distribution.

a. Subharmonic   b. Digital room correction
c. Robinson-Dadson curves   d. Frequency

49.   The fundamental tone, often referred to simply as the fundamental and abbreviated f_o or F_o, is the lowest frequency in a
harmonic series.

The _____ of a periodic signal is the inverse of the pitch period length. The pitch period is, in turn, the smallest repeating unit of a signal.

a. 1-center problem

b. Fundamental frequency

c. 2-3 heap

d. 120-cell

Chapter 1

1. c	2. d	3. b	4. a	5. d	6. c

Chapter 2

1. c	2. d	3. d	4. d	5. a	6. a	7. d	8. d	9. c	10. d
11. d	12. c	13. b	14. d	15. d	16. a	17. b	18. d	19. b	20. d
21. d	22. d	23. b	24. a	25. a	26. c	27. b	28. d	29. b	30. d
31. d									

Chapter 3

1. c	2. d	3. b	4. d	5. d	6. d	7. d	8. d	9. b	10. d
11. d	12. d	13. d	14. b	15. b	16. d	17. c	18. d	19. d	20. d
21. d	22. a	23. d	24. d	25. c	26. d	27. d	28. c	29. c	30. c
31. d	32. b	33. d	34. d	35. b	36. a	37. d	38. d	39. d	40. b
41. d	42. d	43. a	44. d	45. c	46. a	47. c	48. d	49. d	50. d

Chapter 4

1. a	2. d	3. a	4. c	5. b	6. b	7. d	8. a	9. d	10. d
11. b	12. d	13. d	14. d	15. d	16. d	17. d	18. d	19. b	20. d
21. a	22. d	23. d	24. a	25. d	26. a	27. a	28. d	29. c	30. d
31. d	32. d	33. c	34. d	35. d					

Chapter 5

1. d	2. d	3. d	4. d	5. d	6. c	7. a	8. d	9. c	10. c
11. a	12. d	13. d	14. b	15. b	16. c	17. a	18. d	19. c	20. d
21. d	22. d	23. b	24. d	25. d	26. d	27. c	28. d	29. d	30. a
31. d	32. d	33. d	34. a	35. d	36. d	37. b	38. c	39. a	40. d
41. c	42. d	43. d	44. d	45. d	46. c	47. d	48. a	49. d	50. b
51. d	52. a	53. a	54. d	55. d	56. b	57. d			

Chapter 6

1. d	2. c	3. a	4. d	5. d	6. d	7. a	8. d	9. d	10. d
11. c	12. d	13. d	14. b	15. d	16. d	17. c	18. d	19. b	20. d
21. a	22. a	23. a	24. b	25. d	26. d	27. d	28. d	29. b	30. d
31. d	32. d	33. a	34. d	35. d	36. d				

Chapter 7

1. a	2. d	3. b	4. a	5. b	6. a	7. a	8. b	9. d	10. d
11. a	12. a	13. a	14. d	15. b	16. d	17. a	18. a	19. c	20. b
21. c	22. b	23. d	24. c	25. c	26. d	27. c	28. b	29. c	30. a
31. a	32. d	33. d	34. d	35. c					

Chapter 8

1. c	2. a	3. c	4. b	5. d	6. d	7. d	8. a	9. d	10. c
11. a	12. d	13. d	14. d	15. d	16. a	17. b	18. d	19. b	20. c
21. d	22. b	23. d	24. d	25. a	26. d	27. d	28. d	29. a	30. b
31. c	32. c	33. d	34. b	35. c	36. c	37. d	38. d	39. c	40. a
41. d	42. d	43. b	44. d	45. b	46. a	47. d	48. d	49. d	50. d
51. d	52. d	53. d	54. a	55. b	56. d	57. c			

Chapter 9

1. c	2. d	3. d	4. d	5. d	6. d	7. b	8. d	9. d	10. c
11. d	12. a	13. a	14. c	15. a	16. d	17. d	18. a	19. d	20. c
21. d	22. a	23. d	24. d	25. d	26. c	27. b	28. d	29. d	30. b
31. c	32. d	33. d	34. c	35. d	36. d	37. d	38. d	39. a	40. d
41. b	42. d	43. d	44. d	45. d	46. d	47. a	48. d	49. b	50. c
51. d	52. b	53. d	54. d	55. d					

Chapter 10

1. a	2. a	3. d	4. a	5. d	6. a	7. a	8. d	9. d	10. b
11. c	12. c	13. d	14. b	15. a	16. a	17. a	18. d	19. d	20. d
21. c	22. b	23. a	24. d	25. a	26. d	27. d	28. d	29. d	30. d
31. d	32. c	33. d	34. d	35. d	36. b	37. d	38. a	39. d	40. c
41. c	42. d	43. c	44. d	45. a	46. a	47. d	48. d	49. b	

CPSIA information can be obtained
at www.ICGtesting.com
Printed in the USA
BVHW011731240820
587199BV00006B/179